Approach to Monasticism

APPROACH
TO
MONASTICISM

Dom Hubert van Zeller

SHEED and WARD—New York

To the monks of our Lady of
New Clairvaux, California

Preface

In case it should be feared that this book will turn out to be a condensed version of *The Holy Rule, notes on St. Benedict's legislation for monks,* the claim can be justly made here that what follows is not material put in but material left out of the larger work. Indeed, if it is of the slightest interest to anyone to know it, both *The Holy Rule* and *The Yoke of Divine Love* are themselves digests of what were planned on a more voluminous scale. So apart from its extracts from St. Benedict's Rule and a few re-statements of Benedictine principle, the present volume can be viewed as a fresh approach.

Several reasons have prompted the arrangement, not resorted to in the other four essays of this series, of dividing the book into two parts. The first book looks at the life from the outside, not only as though through the eyes of an applicant from the world, or of a beginner in the cloister, but also as though judging monasticism on its exterior rather than on its interior merits. The second book assumes the problems of the professed rather than those of the postulant. Also it relates to the less obvious aspects of the monastic life. But the division is a loose one. There is much in the earlier section (so the author hopes) that is concerned with the strictly interior life and would be applicable to monks at any stage of their monastic lives. Moreover there is much in the later section that aims at giving a picture of monasticism to the enquiring layman. Books on serious subjects have a way of appearing less formidable when the subject-matter is grouped: the hesitating reader is encouraged to believe that he may skip.

Lastly, and to prevent a misunderstanding of the title, it is neither the history nor the philosophy of monasticism that is at issue here; the avenue of approach is frankly practical and vocational.

Contents

PREFACE   vii

Book I: Approach from the Outside

1. The Project Taken Seriously   5
2. The Response Proved Genuine   19
3. Development According to Rule   47
4. Development According to Prayer   61
5. Deviations to be Denied   87

Book II: Approach from the Inside

6. Simplicity of Vision   105
7. The Work of Solitude   115
8. The Specifically Monastic Virtues   129
9. The Inwardness of the Vows   141
10. The Consequences of Fidelity   173

Approach to Monasticism

BOOK ONE

Approach from the Outside

1

The Project
Taken Seriously

MONASTICISM has come to be a subject which people today discuss. It is no longer something which only the well-informed Catholic knows anything about and on the interpretation of which only monks and nuns have a right to express a view. But so long as it amounts to no more for lay people than a topic of conversation, monasticism is not justifying itself in the service of lay people. What benefits the world is not the knowledge of monasticism's existence but the fact of monasticism's practice. The help which the world receives from monasticism is brought about by the prayer and work of those who are dedicated to God in the monastic vows. Monks influence the world not directly by acquainting people with information but indirectly by fidelity to the monastic purpose.

In the same way for the monks themselves it is not the history or philosophy of monasticism that helps the work of monasticism among them but the actual pursuit of the monastic ideal. Monasticism, its principles and its policies, is meant to be more than a matter of discussion to a monk; it is meant to be a matter of decision. But though experimental knowledge is the knowledge which the monk most needs to acquire, the process of acquisition must be deliberate and not merely passive and automatic.

One reason why there are in monasteries souls whose lives seem never to have taken shape, monks who are spiritually unsettled and undecided and immature from the novitiate onwards, is that for them the monastic life has never got beyond either pure theory or external practice: they have never made up their minds about monasticism, they have never taken it on as a unity. They have entered, rather than chosen, the monastic life. They have not given their whole lives to it, or brought it fully into their lives; they have existed under vows.

You cannot live a life properly until you take it on in its own terms. People who have never given a thought to the Christ-life, whose standards are unchristian, cannot suddenly pick up the Christian ethic as a stick with which to hit their atheist opponents. Either to live a life or to fight a life, you have to be alive at every point of contact with that life. Familiarity with the idea is not enough. The thing has to be taken for what it claims to be, has to be verified, has to be chosen or rejected.

What, then, does monasticism claim to be, and what are its credentials? To each of these questions a variety of answers could be given. A Benedictine authority has said recently that the whole burden of the holy Rule amounts to nothing more and nothing less than the elimination of self-will. So long as you are not following your own desire you are bearing witness to the authenticity and effectiveness of monasticism. Surely this gives a very restricted presentation.

The uprooting of self is part, certainly, of St. Benedict's intention; but monasticism does not consider its work done when it has got men into the way of uprooting. By far the greater part of St. Benedict's plan is concerned with cultivation. The design of the monastic life, from such basic ideas as enclosure and silence down to such minor observances as keeping custody of the eyes when walking about the monastery, is directed towards the love of God. The pressure of the monastic life is not that of the leaden weight, reducing the material of man's will to an even level, but rather that of the tide or current which carries the human will along with it to its fullest natural and supernatural expression.

There is much, as we shall see, that is rightly repressive about monastic observance, but the observance that has more in it of repression than of momentum is doomed to failure. If elimination of self-will were the end aimed at, a man might just as well stay on in the world and act against his inclination whenever he felt inclined to anything. He does not have to enter

7

a monastery in order to block his desires. What happens when his desires happen to coincide with the desires of God? Must he block them? It is often through the soul's desires that God makes known his will. A man comes into a monastery in order to purify his own desires so that he desires only the desires of God. He leaves the world because he realizes that in the world the will of God will not be as clear to him as in the monastery, and above all he wants to see and know in order to love. Monasteries were invented neither to keep people out of mischief nor to keep people happy, but to keep people trying to be good.

The approach to monasticism is only the approach to Christianity through a narrower door. The end is the same, namely union with God. Where the man in the world, guided by grace, has to devise a technique of his own for searching after truth, the monk, also of course guided by grace, can make use of the particular way which his Rule marks out for him. In that they are both trying to respond to whatever light they get from God, the man in the world and the man in the monastery are doing the same thing. It is simply that the man in the monastery is trying to ensure a more single-minded attention to the work. The monastic vocation is nothing else than the grace to choose the way which seems the most sure. If the vocation were to matrimony, it would be the married state that would appear to the subject the most sure.

8

From what has been said it may be noted that the three traditional stages of perfection are reflected in the monastic ideal. Under obedience to his abbot, and following out the ascetical principles which he finds in the Rule, the monk repudiates so far as he can the claims of self: this corresponds to the way of purgation. Answering to graces of monastic prayer, whether coming to him through the liturgy or contemplation, the monk draws nearer to truth as revealed to him in every aspect of his life: this corresponds to the illuminative way. In the faithful contemplation of truth, and helped by the common life which increasingly unifies him in charity, the monk comes to find that the supernatural is replacing the natural and that his own will is losing itself in God's will: this corresponds to the unitive way.

The monastic ideal fulfils also the conditions for perfection outlined in the first psalm where again the three traditional stages are represented. "Blessed the man who hath not walked in the counsel of the godless, nor stood in the way of sinners": the renunciation of the world and of corrupt self. "But his will is in the law of the Lord, and on his law he shall meditate day and night": the search and the enlightenment. "He shall be like a tree that is planted near the running waters . . . and whatsoever he shall do shall prosper": establishment in God and the fruition of such union.

Substitution of the divine for the human; the deepening of charity; union. These are not three separate ends proposed by the monastic ideal but are three aspects of the same end. The monk's life has no other meaning but to tend towards union with God. Apart from this, any other perfection which he may achieve is without value. Whatever his influence for good among souls, whatever his work in the intellectual order, whatever his contribution as an administrator of men and in handling the things of God, the monk is to judge himself monastically—that is, in the light of monasticism's final end, which is the perfect union of the soul with God.

Thus all the monk's valuations and policies, as shown not only in the moment-to-moment occasions but in the settled habits of thought, must be referred to the bar of this primary purpose. To make all decisions in relation to that initial approach is the only way of bearing witness to the seriousness and the sacredness of what has been undertaken. Ultimately it is the only test of the monk's perfection. The monk who makes divine love his goal, who perseveres in his search for it among the other claims to his interest, who is found at the end of his life to be still placing his whole happiness and desire and hope in God's will, has justified both his own vocation and the monastic system.

Such an orientation of mind is not arrived at merely by the act of putting on the habit, nor is it maintained merely by wearing it. Just as the fulness of what the monastic life offers has to be chosen, so the aim of the monastic life has to be repeatedly re-stated. This does not mean that the monk will have to renew, explicitly and at regular intervals, his intention of mounting by God's grace the three stages of perfection to the final consummation; it means that as the occasions present themselves he will express the direction of his desire by choosing according to the ideal.

In practice he will find himself applying the principle all day long. Without undue introspection, and without preoccupation with the side of the life which stresses negation, he will come to judge between the interests which bring him closer to his object and those which stand in the way. He will know how to steer a course among the affections, and how to distinguish between necessary and unnecessary concessions. Does smoking promote my sanctification or is it frankly an indulgence? Do I read a novel because without light literature my progress towards union with God is slowed down, or simply because I like reading novels? Can the money, time, and attention that I give to learning news about the outside world be justified on the grounds that I am as a result a better monk—more recollected, zealous, single-minded?

As a private individual in the community a monk subjects himself to such enquiries, but as a member of the community he has a further responsibility towards the end proposed in the monastic ideal. Acting along

11

the same line as before he will have to assure himself—when it comes to a question of voting, for example, or officially expressing an opinion—that what is projected is truly conducive to the common perfection. If as the superior he has the power to decide the issue for the rest of the community, he will have to look closer still to the prime purpose of monasticism.

A man must choose, then, and it is the choosing that makes him what he is. A community must choose, and again it is by the direction of its choosing that it qualifies as a monastic community. It is a common fallacy, and one of the spiritual dangers of our age, to imagine that by drifting along on the current in which we find ourselves we can always be sure of doing the will of God. While it is true that God normally manifests his will to us through the circumstances of the present moment, it is still true that where these contingencies are found to depart from his intention as made explicit in the terms of the monastic goal—where, in other words, there is a discrepancy between the essence of the holy Rule and its current interpretation—it is the monk's responsibility to take stock of the existing practice and compare it with the original postulate. Observance may not be the whole of monasticism, but it is as good a pointer as any to the authenticity of its spirit.

Our nature possesses this defect, that we do not like making up our minds if we can get someone else to do it for us. In the eighteenth and nineteenth centuries the highly developed spiritual direction which was thought necessary went far to supply souls with the excuse for not making up their minds. But now that confessors are less ready to think of themselves as interpreters of God's design it has become usual to assume, as being the surest way of finding God's will, an attitude of passivity. So long as I do not make up my mind I am safe. If I choose anything but what actually is—so runs the argument—I am expressing self. From such a state of mind spring frustrated vocations which leave souls to follow unhappy careers in the world as well as unwise professions which cause unhappiness in the monastery.

Very often the price of not facing the problem in the beginning is to find oneself saddled later on with the same problem, which now admits of no solution. A man, on the too facile assumption that God's will is infallibly to be found in the existing state, stays on in the world when he should be in a monastery; his aspirations continue, but, because he becomes committed to a family, admit of no appropriate satisfaction. A novice, with leanings to a different form of religious life from that which obtains in the monastery where he is making his trial, goes through to profession—again on the assumption that God's will is infallibly seen in the set of surrounding circumstances—and thus stores up problem-material which will mount with the years. A community which tentatively launches out into an activity which calls for decisions and safeguards, finds itself, having neglected the restrictions on the grounds that God's will must be allowed to work its way, so deeply involved as to be now unable to limit the demands upon its essential life as a monastery.

On this latter point the most obvious examples would be those of apostolic and educational activities. Thus a community might with justification undertake to evangelize the immediate neighborhood, and find itself eventually drained of manpower for the choir; the policy has been declared and the precedents established; there is no going back. Or the work of retreats for lay people has been embarked upon, and before the implications have been fully grasped, the silence and routine of the house have been sacrificed. In the field of education the demands are, if anything, more pressing and searching. It is not that the contemplative ideal is compromised by the act of taking a few classes and having a few boys under the care of selected monks. This was allowed for by St. Benedict and has fairly consistent Benedictine tradition to justify it. The problem arises when this small-scale conception of education gives place to the idea of running a large modern school where the work is necessarily competitive and secular. In order to equip the young with all that justice both to their parents and to their future careers requires, the modern school must put material ambitions well to

14

the fore. The purely spiritual welfare of those entrusted to the monks is not the sole care. The monks who teach may be contemplatives, but it is not as contemplatives that they are employed in the work of teaching. The order to which they belong may be contemplative, but it is not because of this that parents send their children to the Benedictines. The question presents itself in this form: are we to assume that both the size and the secular nature of the modern Benedictine school must necessarily be the will of God?

It would be interesting if we could know what future religious historians will be saying about us, and whether they will charge the present era with getting its values wrong. We, too close to the scene for an accurate judgment of perspectives, are inclined to think that the threat to the Church's traditional ways is coming from something outside, from the pressure of dialectical materialism and the totalitarian system, when possibly a more dangerous enemy comes from within, from a want of right emphasis. At various levels there exists the illusion that better results can be obtained by doing a work which is not one's own but someone else's. Contemplative orders are lured into doing the work of active orders; active orders are lured into doing the work of laymen; laymen are lured into running social societies to the neglect of prayer. The highest motives do not guarantee the highest standards, and all along the line a loss is suffered. Such a loss would not be suffered if the contemplative orders confined the overflow of contemplation to study, to giving retreats, to instructing and helping souls from within the enclosure; and if the active orders took on no more than their rules and constitutions demanded.

Certainly man must always help man for the love of God, even at the price of having to sacrifice something of the more immediate service of God in solitude and prayer, but he must help man in the way God wants and not in the way he thinks God ought to want. From the way people argue it might be thought that if he knew as much about the modern world as we do, God would think differently about the work of religious orders. "Live according to what you are and you develop": *not* to live according to what you are is not only to impoverish your own life but also to deprive others of their life-blood, which is prayer. As cells in the mystical body we receive and communicate life not physically but spiritually. We make a fatal mistake when, on the grounds of giving more abundant life and giving it more directly, we impoverish one limb in order to minister to another. The limbs minister to one another in Christ, and to play an independent part for the good of his body is to assume that we are indispensable to the good of his body: it is to show a lack of faith in his power to help his own body.

The approach to monasticism, then, resolves itself into the approach to the will of God. The attitude must be at once realist and idealist: realist in the sense of facing the fact of our own limitations, of contemporary conditions, of never being quite able to see letter and spirit and observance in unity; idealist in the sense of having infinite confidence in the power of grace, and of being ready always to follow such light as will show us more of truth. God's will is his truth, which is our goal. If our intention is restricted to looking for a part of truth, and to doing only some of his will, we can hardly call ourselves complete monks: we are answering to only half of our vocation. Nor if we follow only some of the principles of our Rule, or else follow all of them but in an accommodated sense, do we qualify as complete monks.

"To have a degree of regard for God and yet not to act wholly for the sake of God," says St. Bernard, speaking to monks, "is the mark of a soul that is insincere. If the intention is directed towards God chiefly because of the necessities of the present life, this may not indeed be insincerity, but it is mark of lowness and feebleness of heart and is far from being acceptable to God. Further, to direct the mind towards some object other than God, though it be for the sake of God, is not the repose of Mary but the care and trouble of Martha."[1]

[1] *Sermons on the Canticle,* 40.

17

2

The Response
Proved Genuine

FOR THE SAKE of sequence let it be supposed that the layman, distinguishing between the true and false doctrine about the will of God, has broken away from the circumstances which surrounded him in the world and has joined a monastic community. He has assessed his natural, and so far as possible his spiritual, qualities; he has balanced against one another the attractions of different congregations and different monasteries; he has read the holy Rule and prayed for light; he has applied at the monastery of his choice and has been accepted; and here he is—a novice. What now? May he leave the question of his vocation in the hands of his superiors, or is the responsibility still as much his as it was before he entered? May he assume that if he is called to some other form of life he will be sent away from this one, or must he go on raking his soul in search of the will of God?

To answer this very common problem it is necessary only to point to the nature of the novitiate, which is to give both novice and novicemaster a share in the burden of decision. Thus it would be just as much a mistake for the novice to feel bound to proceed to profession unless ordered to leave as it would be for the novicemaster to feel bound to advise him for profession if the novice did not leave of his own accord. In each case it would mean a misunderstanding both of the purpose of the novitiate and of the way in which God means us to learn his will.

A novice has not taken a vow of stability, and for him or for the novicemaster to act on the assumption that God's will must lie in following the course without thought of change, and that if a change should be willed by God it would be effected irrespective of novice and novicemaster, is to act superstitiously. What are novitiates for ? Has freewill no bearing on the will of God, and has the will of God no bearing on freewill? It is no compliment to God to tell him that he must work a miracle to make us do what he is already giving us the grace to do ourselves.

Once he has made his vows it is a very different story, but the novice who persuades himself that his serious attraction to another form of monastic life is nothing but a temptation stops on in the novitiate not because he is following the light to stay but because he is following the absence of a light to stay. God's will is more likely to be seen in a considered and steady attraction towards a spiritual object than in the lack of attraction of any kind. Before the desire for a greater good can be sacrificed to the possession of a lesser and present good, it must be proved beyond doubt that the good in hand outweighs, in God's sight, the good proposed. Such a proof may be provided by the fact of profession, but to sacrifice the aspiration on nothing more than the dictum *melior est conditio possidentis* is not so much to play for safety as to play for stagnation.

Those for their part whose duty it is to advise the novice have corresponding obligations. Only if their judgments are free of prejudice and doctrinaire ruling can they expect to distinguish between a soul's true and false attraction, between the true and false apprehension of the will of God. A novicemaster or confessor, taking it as axiomatic that novices must always be pressed to persevere, will sometimes make too little allowance for the individual action of grace. He will perhaps not sufficiently take into account the effect of the novitiate in opening up new spiritual interests to a soul hitherto immersed in affairs. People are apt to change a good deal in a novitiate, and an adviser who bases his advice on a knowledge of the novice as he was before he came into the monastery may well be misled. Perhaps the novice is at last discovering his true self, and had he not entered the novitiate he might not have realized his bent for the interior life which is now drawing him towards a more enclosed and contemplative form of monasticism. Who is the adviser to tell him that if it were not God's will that profession should be made here, in this monastery and no other, God would not have brought him to it in the first place? God does not pledge himself to give, all at once, the whole of a vocation. Like any other grace, the grace of vocation is a moment-to-moment affair. The ways in which it can be lost suggest that this is so. Certainly in many cases God seems, without committing himself, to give to souls the vocation of trying their vocation. Though the particular monastery where the experiment is made would normally be the monastery of subsequent profession, there is nothing in the Rule to say that it must be.

Nor would it be fair on the part of the novicemaster or director to urge upon the novice the claim of blind faith in his vocation to this particular community, telling him that such an act of absolute trust calls for greater perfection than any which might be found in an objectively more perfect way of life. The director is not there to tell him what heroic things he can do if he sets his mind to it, but simply to help him to discover the will of God. There are those too, and with less justification, who try to keep novices from straying to other houses by outlining to them an idealized future in their own. "If you only have patience and stop on with us," they tell the hesitating novice, "you will live to see your monastic aspirations fulfilled. That is why God has given them to you, so that you should be able to help in furthering the spirit which is already stirring. If all who felt as you and I do were to leave, what would be the future of the house? But, take my word for it, the day will come when there can be had here all that any of your stricter monasteries can offer." It is no part of the director's work to assume the prophet's mantle. Just as it is for the novice to consider taking vows in the monastery as it is, and not in the monastery as it might be, so it is for the professed monk who is consulted to come forward with facts and the fruit of experience, not with fancies and misleading enthusiasms.

It is always, then, for the director and the directed alike, a question of finding out what God wants in the given instance. For this a great detachment and flexibility will be required. Vocation is not the call which a man would send out to men like him if he were God; it is the call which in fact God does send out to this particular man. The whole problem resolves itself into hearing it right. Of the soul groping for light in this matter of vocation St. Bernard says: "Although he is occupied about good things, he feels a grave uncertainty between the claims of fruitful labour and of restful contemplation . . . from one moment to another he entreats with tears and sighs to be shown the will of God. In these uncertainties the one and only remedy is the work of prayer and the frequent raising of the soul to God, asking that he would deign to make continually known to us what we ought to do, and when and how we ought to do it."[1]

[1] *Sermons on the Canticle,* 57.

Though there is no generalizing about vocations, St. Benedict in his fifty-eighth chapter is prepared to give four signs which ordinarily accompany the genuine monastic vocation. He instructs the novicemaster to "examine whether the novice truly seeks God, and whether he is zealous for the *opus Dei*, for obedience, and for humiliations." If these qualities in the novice do not altogether prove that God is calling him to the monastic state, and still less to this particular monastery rather than to any other, the absence of these qualities can safely be taken to disprove it.

The mark mentioned first by St. Benedict, *si revera Deum quaerit*, if he truly seeks God, has been largely dealt with above in connection with light upon God's will. St. Benedict wants the novicemaster to assure himself that the applicant for profession is clear about the difference between God's will and his own. If a man begins his religious life confusing God's will with what he wants God's will to be, he will end it by doing nothing but his own will and calling it God's.

While it is impossible for a soul to be wholly disinterested in the search for God, it is possible to avoid dissimulation. What St. Benedict wants to see before all else in those who make trial of the monastic life is truth. No future training in the ways of monasticism can be effectual where integrity is lacking. Whatever his failings in other directions, the novice must show at least a single-minded desire for God.

24

Writers on the religious life are fond of telling us that the monk who looks for anything apart from God in the monastery will be disappointed, that the monastery offers nothing but God, and that God alone gives meaning to the life. Certainly it seems to be true that to become a monk wanting the best of both worlds brings neither natural nor supernatural happiness, but is it quite true to say that the man of mixed ambitions cannot somehow get by as a monk? Indeed that is just the trouble—there *is* enough in the monastic life, apart from the one idea of pleasing God, to keep a man reasonably occupied and interested. Disappointed he inevitably will be, and without God as the abiding inspiration and primary purpose his vocation will in fact be meaningless, but it would be wrong to say that the monastery offered to such a man no consolations save those that could be found in the interior of life. If the matter were as clear as this, the problem of vocation would be a simple one. But it is precisely because a man when about to take vows is faced with such a wealth of good things which he may legitimately desire that so great care must be taken to discover *si revera Deum quaerit.*

The man himself, let alone the novicemaster, may not know how far this condition is being verified. How can I tell if I want God only? How can I be sure that my attraction to the monastic life is not, as much as it is a desire for God, an attraction to security, order, com-

panionship, aestheticism, escape? Though I am too close
to my own nature to be able to see my own motives, I
am not too close to the monastic life to be able to see
its own evaluations. I may be doubtful about my attraction, but I need not be doubtful about my direction.
And *si revera Deum quaerit* relates to the direction of
the will and not to the appeal of the senses nor to the
instinct of self-realization.

If in questions of prayer, penance, works of charity,
it is impossible to be sure of the extent to which earthly
considerations come in, so it is also in the question of
embracing the religious life. But since in prayer, penance, works of charity, the purity of intention is measured by the choice of the will, so also in the matter of
responding to the grace of vocation it is the will which
is the determining factor. I may feel drawn to the
monastic life because of a hundred things about it
which my natural tastes find congenial, but if I choose
the monastic life because of the one thing which my soul
desires, I am satisfying St. Benedict's first condition.

"So that the mind craves to please God only, and is
able to attach itself simply to him," says St. Bernard,
"there is particular need for the pure heart of David,
who said to God: 'My soul cleaved unto thee, O Lord,'
and also, 'It is good for me to stick close unto God.' In
beholding God he was drawn near to him, and in drawing near to him he beheld him."[2] It is by prayer, then,

[2] *Op. cit.*, 7.

that the soul comes to purity of intention. St. Benedict's *si revera Deum quaerit* is in effect guaranteed by prayer, of which it is itself the expression.

It is prayer moreover that keeps the soul choosing consistently, and persevering in the search. The act of choice is something more, in the present context, than a single formulated intention; it is a continued activity. To be effective, the desire to will God's will must become a habit, must be the constant orientation of the soul. Otherwise it is merely a consoling formula. Through all the multifarious benefits of the monastic life the soul must have the pointer set towards God alone. It is when these multifarious benefits are pursued independently, as ends excusably to be desired, that the condition *si revera Deum quaerit* is infringed. If a man does not truly seek God when he comes to the monastery, he might just as well come for the cut of the vestments or the cooking.

The second indication that a man has the makings of a Benedictine is his feeling for the divine office: *si sollicitus est ad opus Dei*, whether he is zealous for the work of God. The order suggests that this second note arises out of the first: the soul whose whole effort in the monastery is directed towards pleasing God will want to express that effort in the form of liturgical prayer. The *opus Dei* is intended by St. Benedict to be the focus-point of the monk's life, the concentration of activity which justifies his leaving behind him the social responsibilities and apostolic opportunites which would have been his in the world. The vocation to offer public praise to God is a thing in itself, is its own reason for existing, needs no side-line work for souls to vindicate its claims. Since monastic choirs do their work in the name of the mystical body, it is the monastic assumption, verified by the Church's tradition as well as by repeated papal assurances, that the *opus Dei* is no less apostolic than the service which ministers directly to souls.

If the work of liturgical praise is the chief work of the professed monk—*nihil operi Dei praeponatur*, let nothing be preferred to the work of God—the novice will need to get his ideas right about it from the start. His approach to monasticism is expected to be a liturgical approach. This need not mean that a man comes to the cloister by way of the choir; it means that in coming to the cloister a man learns how all his labours as a monk, whether performed in the cell, field, library, or anywhere else, are set to the rhythm of the divine office of which they are the echo.

His appreciation for the *opus Dei* will show itself primarily in the monk's interior life, which will tend to draw its inspiration, implicitly if not explicitly, from the Word. Books and methods of prayer will give place to a more contemplative exercise which derives its impulse from, and at the same time finds its appropriate expression in, the liturgy. Mental prayer becomes an extension, without words, of the act performed when using the medium of words, in choir.

The outward effect of the monk's appreciation for the *opus Dei* will show itself in a number of ways besides that of fidelity to his choirstall. He will take trouble to find out the implications as well as the literal meaning of the psalms, lessons, and hymns; he will apply the strictest self-discipline in the actual rendering of the chant, recitation, ceremonial; he will be ready to give an account of the liturgy's function in the life of the Church to those who consider it to be a waste of time when Christianity is crying out for missionary activity.

On the negative side, too, the monk's indifference to the *opus Dei* will betray itself. He will find good reasons for absenting himself, and when he comes he will arrive late; he will take greater care over consulting the *ordo*, polishing his glasses, finishing his dressing under the cover of his cowl, than over the work which he has come into the choir to do; he will shuffle through his hebdomadal duties, make perfunctory satisfaction for mistakes, stand and sit and look about as though at a party. In those monasteries where the custom of half-choirs is observed he will avail himself of the dispensation's every advantage, regarding it as a privilege to be legitimately excluded from the *opus Dei* instead of accepting the phenomenon in the spirit of faith, humility, and obedience.[3]

The Benedictine who admits that the liturgy means little to him is virtually admitting that his vocation as a monk, his mission as an apostle, his responsibility as a member of the Church mean little to him. Since the obligation of rendering the debt of public homage to the Father is laid particularly upon monastic communities, the monk who fails in the specific work of his community is failing not only his own brethren but the Church as well. The life of the mystical body, since it is the life of Christ, is lived in continuous praise of the Father: failure through lack of interest on the part of the specially deputed members of the mystical body to contribute to that act of praise is a failure in charity in each of its activities. The harmony of worship cannot but be disturbed by the weakening and flattening of individual notes.

"I entreat you," said St. Bernard, who was so devoted to the *opus Dei* that even when seriously ill he insisted on coming to choir, and who used to cross over from his side to the other when he judged his brethren opposite to be flagging, "I entreat you always to occupy yourselves in the praises of God with earnest minds and

[3] The "half-choirs" mentioned here and elsewhere is the system by which alternate sides of the choir are responsible for the maintenance of the *opus Dei*. Each half takes its daily turn, the half which is absent saying office privately.

pure hearts. With earnestness, so as to present yourselves willingly, gladly, reverently at the worship of the
Lord . . . with purity, so as to be always capable, by his
holy inspiration, of making your wills conformable to
his divine will."[4]

Si sollicitus est ad obedientiam, whether he is zealous
for obedience. In making zeal for obedience the third
requirement of the novice, St. Benedict is developing
the original demand that God be sought before all else.
If a man truly seeks God, he will want to surrender
himself to the will of one who represents God. The
superior, whether issuing his own commands or applying the precepts of the Rule, will stand for supernatural
authority. Far from feeling constrained by submission
to a fellow human being, the subject will feel free: surrender to God, whether or not God's power is delegated,
must make for freedom. Freedom is being able to do
God's will; slavery is not being able to master one's own.
But monks should love obedience not because it
makes for a greater sense of liberty but because it makes
for a greater perfection. *"Abdicatio propriae voluntatis
per obedientiam,"* says St. Thomas, *"est via ad perfec-
tionem."*[5] The perfection to which obedience leads the
way is not loved because it represents an achievement

[4] *Op. cit.*, 47.
[5] "The renunciation of self-will by obedience is the way to
perfection."—*Opusc.* 18, c. 10.

31

but because it represents charity. *"Caritas sine obedientia,"* says St. Thomas in another place, *"esse non potest."*[6] When the soul has come to realize that the only thing that matters is pleasing God, and has decided to go the quickest way about it, there appears one very straight course to follow: with obedience the soul cannot go wrong. Once charity has been made the sole aim, obedience is sought for by the soul rather as a means of expression than as a means of discipline. Discipline will not be lacking—subjection of the will for the love of God is the highest form of penance—but instead of being seen as superimposed from without it will be seen as elicited from within.

As in the case of zeal for the *opus Dei,* zeal for obedience will show itself outwardly in a number of ways. Apart from the clear-cut occasions presented in the ordinary run of religious life—occasions when the subject's readiness to fulfil the superior's command is shown by promptitude, cheerfulness, exactitude—there are the borderline occasions which will test the delicacy of the monk's response. Thus the fully obedient monk will welcome general recommendations, personal suggestions, corrections in public and private; he will offer himself for those less agreeable duties which might otherwise fall to someone else; he will interpret strictly, and to his disadvantage, questions of permission and

[6] "Charity without obedience cannot exist." *Summa,* II-II, q. 104, a. 3, c. fin.

dispensation; in the matter of respect due to authority he will subject his thought as well as his conversation to scrutiny.

On the negative side, again as in the case of the *opus Dei*, the monk who is deficient in this particular zeal will give himself away. *Si sollicitus est ad opus Dei, ad obedientiam.* Where the *opus Dei* is belittled there are complaints that it takes too long and wastes time; where obedience is weak there are complaints that superiors expect too much and waste their subjects' talents on unsuitable undertakings. Criticism, whether of the liturgy as anachronistic or of the superior as incompetent, is the sign that the soul has not fully surrendered to the Benedictine ideal. Once a man yields completely, he takes the forms presented to him by the life. If he has recognized his vocation as coming from the Holy Spirit, the monk knows the truth of St. Thomas's *totum bonum hominis consistit in subjectione ad Deum,*[7] and sees in both the prayer life that is offered to him and in the obedience which is his to offer the means of realizing this subjection.

"Let no one in the monastery follow the will of his own heart," says St. Benedict in his third chapter. For him the virtue of obedience inevitably accompanies, and develops from, humility. The monk who discovers himself to be slipping from St. Benedict's standard of

[7] "The whole good of a man lies in his subjection to God." —*Ibid.,* II-II, q. 18, a. 11.

obedience will know what is wrong: he will recognize the egotism which is making him scornful of rules and recommendations. It is because he is following a *voluntatem proprii cordis*, it is because he is not humble enough, that he makes it difficult for superiors to tell him things, that he is always looking for exemptions, that he pesters authority until he gets what he wants, that he does not finish what is given him to do, that he applies himself only to those works which he enjoys and then does them in his own way. All this is disobedience, but more radically it is pride.

Preaching on the subject of the marriage feast at Cana, St. Bernard takes the sixth and last jar to represent obedience. The implication is that when we have reached the end of the line, filling each jar in its ascending order of importance, we shall be ready for the further grace which changes water into wine. "They had obeyed him," says St. Bernard of the disciples and attendants, "in the hearing of the word. These six water-pots are placed for our cleansing; they are empty if used for mere vainglory." The water-pots by themselves will not save us any more than our rules and constitutions have the power by themselves to save us. "They are filled if observed in the fear of God. Although not tasteful, the fear of God is very refreshing to the soul. And water is changed by divine power into wine when perfect love casts out all fear."[8] Only when

[8] Sermon for the first Sunday after the octave of the Epiphany.

34

our monastic observance is complete, when we have obediently complied with the instructions and filled the jars to the brim, can we reasonably expect the miracle which will turn the dull tasteless material of our service into the joy of divine love. Obedience is the only proof that we really want such a miracle to happen.

The fourth point on which the novicemaster is instructed to assure himself before profession takes place is the novice's acceptance of humiliations. St. Benedict's words are *si sollicitus est ad opprobria,* if he is zealous for humiliations. Just as the monk who is truly obedient looks forward to obediences, so the monk who is truly humble looks forward to humiliations. To be zealous for humiliations, however, is to show one kind of zeal; to be zealous for the *opus Dei* is to show another. A man may feel naturally attracted to praying in choir; nobody feels naturally attracted to looking a fool.

While the choir provides occasions for revealing it, this fourth mark of the Benedictine vocation is more closely related to the first and third marks than to the second. In connection with the first, the monk who truly seeks God will see in his humiliations a reflection of Christ's; in connection with the third, the monk who has surrendered himself by obedience will welcome being trampled on. With Christ whom he seeks he is "made obedient unto death"; he is humiliated unto death.

One reason why it is important to show right from

the start of his monastic life this willingness to be humbled is that as the monk grows older the occasions become both more frequent and more searching. If he has not learned as a novice how to acquit himself under correction, he will not learn later on how to meet slights, indifference, and the humbling loneliness of being passed over in favour of much younger men. The attitude of a monk in middle age towards the inequalities inevitable in community life is to a large extent conditioned by how he bore himself in the novitiate when made to look silly.

Though ridicule may often be simply the criticism of the ill-bred, it may be for the person ridiculed a most valuable experience. Like any other suffering it can drive a man either to bitterness or to Christ. Our instinct when humiliated is to think of the indignity of the situation. But if we were truly humble and had no dignity we would not mind. We would, if we were holy, feel privileged. Christ suffered indignities, but he never spoke of them as indignities. Worthy of infinite honour, he accepted, in silence, dishonour. We, when we are hurt or insulted, at once cry out. If we were to meet with nothing but dishonour all our lives, we would have no grounds for complaint. It is not often that we are falsely accused, but often we are misinterpreted and misquoted. We resent this fiercely as an injustice. Occasionally our weaknesses are exposed, or we are correctly quoted but to our disadvantage. We resent this just as much.

If humility is truth, then the love of humiliation is the love of the evidence of truth. The humble man, the saint, sees in shame something which the rest of us do not see. It is to him at once a witness and an identification: a witness to his worthlessness and an identification with the degradation of Christ. We shrink from humiliation simply because we have never learned the secret beauty of shame with Christ.

Having enumerated the qualities which he wants to see in those who are being trained for the monastic life, St. Benedict immediately goes on to tell the novice-master that "all the hardships and trials by which we travel to God" must be put before the novitiate. Where it might have been expected that St. Benedict would soften his doctrine he is found instead to confirm it. If the demands are felt by the applicant to be too severe, then it is probable that the vocation is lacking. It is better to be dismayed and turned away than to be falsely confident and allowed to stop on.

Some would see in the whole system of monastic self-discipline, and particularly in this matter of being "zealous for humiliations," a streak of the unhealthy. Repression has had its day, they would hold, and the time has come for spirituality to draw even with psychiatry in emancipating the mind from those dreads

37

which are caused either by the sense of guilt or a fear of hardship. Instead of harping on the *dura et aspera* through which we travel to God, St. Benedict would have done better to encourage his novices with thoughts about the sweetness and peace which are to be found on the way. If the rough side of God's service is too frankly presented, the modern novice will look elsewhere. When there is already an obvious beauty in following Christ, is it not a mistake to look for the secret beauty of following him in his shame?

Since the line of objection just quoted calls in question the value of Christian asceticism as a whole, and since the present work is concerned only with the monastic tradition, no attempt will be made here at a large-scale defence.[9] What follows touches only the fringe of the subject, but to have left out all discussion of Benedictine asceticism would have been to ignore an essential element of the Rule.

In the first place the idea that monks must be drawn to God by a silken thread is utter nonsense. The phrase *dura et aspera* is taken directly from Cassian's twenty-fourth conference,[10] and what was the standard authority for western monasticism then can be looked to as the standard authority now. The basic principles of

[9] The case for Christian mortification is given in the first of this series, *Approach to Penance*.

[10] Ch. 25. The same expression is to be found in the *Lausiac History of Palladius*, ch. 41.

monasticism, like the basic principles of religion itself, remain the same. Christianity does not coax the faithful towards the kingdom of heaven, but tells them instead that the kingdom of heaven suffereth violence and that only the violent bear it away. Twice in the Apocalypse we have Christ represented to us as wielding a crook of iron with which to correct his straying flock.[11] Religious communities may not be straying flocks, but they are expected to take correction as though they were. If the Good Shepherd does not do it for them, they are expected to administer it themselves.

One reason why monasteries reach the stage of failing to attract vocations may well be that their appeal to the young is no longer made in terms of *dura et aspera*. Lacking St. Benedict's original appreciations, they hold out new inducements, and are disappointed. But the idea of sacrifice, understood in its hard old-fashioned unambiguous sense, has never failed to draw the young of whatever period, nation, ideology. This is not to suggest that monks should use asceticism as a campaigning point; it is to suggest that if they hope to maintain their monasteries they must be faithful to the whole of St. Benedict's idea and not merely to parts of it. Communities do not have to shout about their asceticism, because it shouts for them. All they have to do is to make sure of not neglecting it. It is not publicity that draws souls, but practice. In the spiritual operation of cause and

[11] Apoc. 12; 5 and 19; 15.

effect, the more hidden the asceticism the greater the influence. There is no more effective propaganda for the monastic life than the combination of penance and prayer practised in obscurity and even in seclusion.

On an earlier page we have seen how the approach to monasticism is the approach to charity. The law of love is a law of negation as well as one of affirmation. Pursuit of the object loved means the rejection of other possible loves, means the repression of every obstacle to love. Love without discipline would not be love at all, but licence. Service without the repression of other possible services would not be service at all, but only one or other form of selfishness. Sacrifice is the expression of love, service, selflessness, and there is no sacrifice where there is no repression.

The idea that repression is always wrong reflects the age and society in which it flourishes. To say that human instincts need to be brought into the open is to assume that human instincts are good and can be left to express themselves in safety. However good they were before the fall, they are not uniformly good now. If the noble instincts that exist in man are to have their way, those that are ignoble must be repressed. To urge the claims of nature's law is to point to only one of nature's rulings; nature as a whole is not self-perfecting. Leave a field of corn to develop itself, and it will become a field of weeds.

The monk takes repression in his stride not because

he likes repressing his instincts but because he loves God. He knows that here is one instinct which must at all cost be followed, so the repression of other instincts is assumed. It is a mistake to think of the monk as waging war on the senses for the sake of aggression. He wages war for the sake of peace—in Christ. Like St. Paul, who "beat his body and made it a slave,"[12] the monk has his eye on liberty rather than on slavery. He is set against the slavery of sin. He hopes that by choosing the less easy course day in and day out—by embracing the *dura et aspera*—he may come to choose the hard way when the course of sin opens easily in front of him. *Then* he will have an instinct he can safely follow: it will be second nature to him to do the less easy thing. This is the liberty which St. Paul was achieving, paying in the currency of repressions the price which has to be paid for the liberty enjoyed by the children of God.

In practice the proof of the argument comes up before us every day. Between choosing as a supporter either a self-controlled or a self-indulgent man we would not hesitate for a moment. Between giving our confidence to a mortified or an immortified monk we would not hesitate for a moment. Between joining a disciplined or undisciplined monastery we would not hesitate for a moment. Living in the senses is no substitute for living in the spirit, and once we have been called in the spirit we are pledged to the spirit. Sense may continue to at-

[12] I Cor. 9; 27.

41

tract us, but it is only the things of the spirit that win our admiration.

Since it is the tendency in man to reduce the standard from the level of spirit to the level of sense, it is the work of grace to counter this decline by raising men's desires from the world of sense to the world of the spirit. Answering to the monastic vocation, a soul becomes well placed to further this work of grace. The combined effects of prayer and solitude make it easier for the monk than for the man in the world, who has not the same opportunity, both to see what repressions are needed and to apply them without a conflict of obligations. The holy Rule, the will of the superior, association with his brethren, the routine of the monastery, the nature of the work that is given to him: all these factors will play their part in indicating to the monk the appropriate repressions to be adopted. But not one of them will play a part unless he lets it. Monastic repressions must be deliberately accepted or they are wasted. There are few things more sad in a monastery—in life outside for the matter of that, but particularly in a monastery—than repressions resented.

If unhappiness is the lot of the sense-centred and self-centred, then happiness as well as holiness must follow the mortification of sense and self. Those outside who think of monastic repressions as leading necessarily to mental tension and neuroses are seeing the subject only in terms of the conflict between appetite and consent, between need and satisfaction, between emotion and determination. To them the ascetic is like a child sitting under a table in the dark while a splendid meal is being served over his head. Why does he not come out of his sulks and join the others at their eating? But the point is that the ascetic is not sulking: he has chosen to sit under the table for the time being, knowing very well that an altogether better sort of meal is being prepared which will be his eventually.

Certainly tension is the result of disunion, but only when there is disunion in the mind. When a man's higher faculties are acting together in denying gratification to the lower faculties, there may be rebellion in the body but there will not be tension in the mind. The mind, composed of intellect and will, is in harmony. Where reason and desire are agreed on a policy, sense can do no more than clamour.

Monastic asceticism, indeed all asceticism, is simply the system which aims at stilling the clamour of the senses by establishing agreement in the mind. The clamour is never entirely stilled, but at least there is a settled attitude towards it. The attitude supposes certain assumptions which the world has never accepted but which have served monasticism well and which even the weakest of monks would not deny. One such assumption is that texts like St. Peter's "I call upon you to be as strangers and exiles, to resist those appetites that war against the soul,"[13] like St. Paul's "Every athlete must keep all his appetites under control; and he does it to win a crown that fades, whereas ours is imperishable,"[14] like St. James's "Wantons, have you never been told that the world's friendship means enmity with God,"[15] are meant to be taken seriously. Another such assumption is, as has been suggested, that weeds do not grow into fruit-trees, and that if fruit is to be expected of it the tree must be pruned at its branches while the soil is loosened at its roots. Much of man is still embedded in the earth, much of man sends out the wrong kind of branch which must be cut off if the significant strength is to be conserved and developed.

It is right that we should feel uncomfortable when we read of St. Benedict's ideas about mortification as outlined in the Rule. Certain passages were clearly meant to make us feel uncomfortable. But perhaps over the centuries the nature of the discomfort has changed, and instead of reading with dread about the *dura et aspera* which we shall have to undertake we read with embarrassment about the *dura et aspera* which we have not undertaken. But even this is salutary; at least it shows that we are not so scornful and sophisticated as to dismiss the whole conception as archaic.

Or it may be that we recognize the necessity of hard-

[13] I Peter 2; 11.
[14] I Cor. 9; 25.
[15] James 4; 4.

ship in the monastic life but give to Saint Benedict's words a purely spiritual application. The spiritual trials, after all, are both more searching and more sanctifying than any form of austerity, so why not concentrate upon the inwardness of St. Benedict's expressions? To this excuse St. Bernard gives us the answer when he says: "Even that outward conversion should not be considered of little moment since it is known to be of no little significance in assisting the conversion which is spiritual."[16] The saint is here commenting on the verse of Joel, *Convertimini ad me in toto corde vestro, in jejunio et fletu et planctu,*[17] and goes on to say of the clause which relates to fasting: "I would remind you, brethren, that it is not from meats only but from all the enticements of the flesh and from all sensual gratification." "If the appetite has sinned," says St. Bernard in another place, "let it fast . . . but if the other members also have sinned, why should they not also fast? Let the eye, which has robbed the soul, fast; let the ear, the hand, the tongue, and the soul fast."[18] St. Bernard had no doubts in interpreting the thought of earlier ascetics, Joel, Cassian, St. Benedict.

Allowing, then, that the challenge of monasticism has been taken up in full seriousness, that some at least of

[16] *Sermon for Lent,* 4.

[17] "Be converted unto me with all your heart, in fasting and weeping and mourning."

[18] *Sermon on the Lenten Fast.*

45

its implications have been seen with wide-eyed honesty, that the response has been verified by the continued search for God, by love of the *opus Dei*, by zeal for obedience and humiliation: what does the soul do next? Willing to meet with hardship, exterior as well as interior, the beginner in monastic life strides out into the observance of the holy Rule. To help him on his way he has the doctrine and advice of his superiors, the example of his fellow monks, the tradition of monasticism. Above all he has the life of Christ to draw from, and the grace to see his monastic service as an adventure of love. He knows that the end of his journey is union. It is by this ideal that his approach to monasticism is charted.

3

Development
According to Rule

To THOSE WHO, when every other scriptural text has been forgotten, will remember that the letter kills whereas the spirit quickens, the idea that monastic perfection can be measured by fidelity to rule will hardly recommend itself. In an age when spiritual writers make liberty of spirit a surer sign of sanctity than almost any other, the doctrine of exact observance as the clearest indication of charity and response to grace finds little favour even among religious. The whole subject of law—its necessity, obligation, effect, division, validity—has been dealt with by countless authorities. In the present chapter, which does not for a moment presume to share the honours with the standard works, a few points about law will be developed which have their bearing particularly upon the unassuming subject of keeping rules.

The principle that if it works for me I can safely follow it, a principle of subjective pragmatism, must necessarily lead to the rejection of accepted norms. Where pressed, it leads to anarchy. In human life, as in physical and natural life, there has to be a rule of order. The rule is imposed, moreover, by something outside the subject and independent of it. The order, or supposed order, inside the subject is not the sole criterion. A farmer does not sow when he feels like it but when the season dictates. The direction of a swallow's flight or of a salmon's course is no more determined by mood than the needle of a compass or of a barometer is moved by something inside itself. There is in each case a law at work, objective and independent of the forces or elements which it governs. Not even the most creative of artists paints a sunset strictly out of his head. There must be *some* norm. For a musician to compose a waltz tune, and for a dancer to dance to it, there must be a recognizable combination of forms. If a sculptor is to carve the human shape, he must observe certain structural conventions. The list could be extended indefinitely.

If then there has to be a standard in the physical and natural order, there has to be a corresponding standard in the moral and spiritual order. Religion in its widest sense has its established objective code; Christianity narrows this down to a more positive and particular law; monasticism narrows it still further with its rule, constitutions, and local observances. The laws of religion, whether in the wider or narrower sense, are often prohibitive in expression, but they are not prohibitive in substance: they prohibit only in order to direct. They follow the course which we have considered in connection with the *dura et aspera;* they help the soul to attain to union with God. Traffic lights were not designed as yet another way of preventing the reckless from transgressing; they were designed to ensure a measure of safety to reckless and cautious alike.

Taking it for granted, then, that the whole system of monastic legislation is constructive rather than preventative or punitive, we come upon the question of observance as we would come upon the question of perfection itself. Observance may not be perfection, but it is one of the best ways of attaining to it. Observance is the standard way because it is the standard index of charity. Charity, which is at once perfection and the way to perfection, has other signs than kindness, compassion, good nature, and hospitality by which it may be judged, and the most trustworthy of these is the sign of obedience. So far as the Rule goes, a monk's observance of the Rule and obedience to the superior are the same thing; it is only when the question of a superior's command comes in that obedience goes on from where observance leaves off.

People speak about monastic observance as though it were a monastic fad. It is in fact the most reliable of monastic credentials. People say of an exact religious that he is scrupulous and even sanctimonious; what they should say is that he has a more delicate perception of obedience and charity than they have. In explaining the process of beatification, the Sacred Congregation has declared that the perfect observance of a religious rule can be taken as evidence of heroic charity. Perfect observance supposes complete surrender of self-will, constant response to grace, the development of the theological virtues together with the gifts of the Holy Ghost. Perfect observance, faithfully persevered in over the years, not only assumes the practice of many virtues, but is itself the continued practice of truth. Conformity is only another name for truth. Conformity in charity and obedience to the pattern proposed by God through the text of the holy Rule is for the monk the highest perfection.

It is true, as we shall see in a later chapter, that observance is not altogether proof against falsehood: it can be devalued by routine, vainglory, lack of proportion. But observance is not alone in this. Every virtue can be given a forged signature. Charity and humility can be so deflected from the true standard as to become nothing but the mask of hypocrisy. Exact observance of the Rule may well screen a number of unpleasant qualities, but it is difficult to see how, given time, the quality of the observance will not prove itself. Either the unpleasant characteristics which are hidden behind punctilious exactitude will give themselves away, or the discipline imposed by the Rule will—by its ideals as well as by its regulations—enable the positive and virtuous elements to dominate. Certainly to maintain an unbroken external observance while inwardly out of tune with the Rule, and without ever betraying one's true self, would be to stretch the act of deception to a degree of almost heroic single-mindedness.

It is a mistake to imagine that in monastic life the choice must be made between being perfectly charitable and being perfectly faithful to rule. A man does not have to choose between seeing out of one or other eye, between walking with one or other leg. Acts of charity and acts of observance are movements of the same activity. They are not two obligations, two loyalties, but one. To see a conflict between sympathy and silence is to admit a lack of unity. Charity, service of God and man, does not divide but on the contrary makes one. If a religious cannot harmonize his fraternal with his disciplinary responsibilities, it means that he has got either his social or his obediential conscience working wrong.

The saints had no difficulty in balancing what they owed to their brethren and what they owed to their Rule. With the saints there was no nonsense about breaking rules for the sake of higher principles. For them the danger of allowing the letter to stifle the spirit did not come up: for them the letter expressed the spirit. This accounts for the meticulous fidelity to rule which we see in the lives of those most possessed by charity. We read of St. Teresa putting outside the door of her cell at night the pins and buttons for which she had not yet been able to get permission, of St. Bernard keeping the monastic regulation about custody of the eyes so strictly as not to notice whatever was above the level of his head, of St. Thomas leaving his desk at the sound of the bell even if it meant not finishing the word he was writing, of St. Anselm returning so abruptly to silence when the rule enjoined it as to leave his discourse hanging in the air: we read of these things and put them down to the edifying eccentricities which we have learned to associate with sanctity. But they are nothing to do with eccentricity: they are the logical outcome of the mind and heart of sanctity.

Christ himself, though subject to no law, was careful to observe the law of the Roman empire. If this was not for necessity it was certainly not for any whim. It was to show us, as his words when under trial were to show us, that authority comes from the Father and that what is laid down by law is to be taken, unless proved contrary to the divine will, as coming from him. Moreover, Christ's representative on earth, Pius XII, said in 1958 that there must be no weakening of religious rules under pressure of prevailing laxity. "The spiritual families consecrated to the Lord must be preserved from the harmful ideas which today tend to ease the chain of obedience, faithfulness to the rule, the spirit of poverty and of self-denial as if they were characteristics of an outdated time . . . while everyone will remain faithful to the rules and customs of his institute, everything will co-operate to the advantage of the Church, especially at this time when the enemy of the name of Christ is mustering his forces against God and against those who serve him."[1]

In periods and countries like our own which have witnessed a sharp rise in the standards of living, the menace to those things which meant much to our fathers and founders is a menace to be countered by extreme measures. Religious observance is always liable to be endangered by either a desire to keep pace with the prevailing standard in the world or a suspicion of the role of strictness in the cloister. It is poverty that falls a victim to the first line of attack; regularity and silence fall victims to the second. The danger would not exist if religious took their stand on the principles and practices of people like St. Bernard, St. Teresa, St. Thomas, St. Anselm, whose interpretations have been cited above. But it is so much easier to talk about adjusting oneself to the conditions and needs of modern life, so much easier to explain one's lax ways by referring to the narrowness of the strict. In all this the failure lies in making the wrong comparisons. It is not for the monastery to compare its standard of living with that of the expensive hotel; not for the monk to compare his lack of discipline with another's lack of propor-

[1] Address of Pope Pius XII to the superiors of all religious orders for men, February 12, 1958.

tion or lack of discretion. For a just comparison there must be a common foundation, and the first thing that should strike one about a monastery is that it is fundamentally different from an establishment in the world; the first thing that should strike one about a monk is that he is living a life which is proportioned—where his perspectives are in order.

The truth is that since monasteries are human institutions, having a natural as well as a supernatural life going on inside them, the idea of returning to a more primitive way of life is disagreeable. Monasteries can adapt themselves without struggle to an existing environment or to an existing emergency; monasteries can envisage a future in which expansion and development prominently figure; what monasteries cannot easily bring themselves to do is to look back at their origins and reshape themselves according to the patterns which they see there. The reformer, except perhaps among a small minority of sabre-rattlers, is not welcomed in monasteries. He is suspect. He is held to be looking for personal advancement, to be animated by bitterness towards his brethren, to be a crank or a neurotic or a rebel. He is seldom given the credit for wanting the will of God and the glory of the order.

Yet down the ages of monastic history the list of reformers is not altogether inglorious. Reformers are only those who have seen an aspect of truth and have fallen in love with it. They are out for conformity to the standard which was set in the original conception. They have seen a deviation and have pledged themselves to correct it. For those who have either themselves deviated or who have suffered the consequences of deviation, the reformer is of course a man who will not mind his own business, an anarchist, an enemy of the existing order. But it is not always safe to deny that he possesses the spirit of God. The reformer may, in the providence of God, be the soul raised up by grace to restore the balance which has been more upset than the majority eye can measure. It may require a man who can be justly charged with seeing only one point of view to bring about a result which would not follow greater circumspection. Too great a circumspection, leading to unnecessary concessions, may have brought about the need for reform. It is a good thing sometimes not to be able to see every point of view. Too many points of view will have the effect of denying enterprise and of obscuring truth. By all means let a man have infinite sympathy for the attitudes of others which he cannot understand, but heaven defend us from the man who will not lift a finger because he sees everyone else's argument.

The authentic spirit of monasticism cannot be expected to flourish outside the recognized frame of monasticism. It is asking a good deal of a Benedictine vocation to set it among circumstances not related to the holy Rule. When we see what care St. Benedict took to surround the monk with all that should bring home to him the supernatural character of his vocation, that should emphasize his separation from the world, that should elicit from him a particular kind of religious service, we begin to understand why the historic reformers of monasticism set such store by the rules of enclosure, silence, external as well as internal obedience, personal as well as corporate poverty. Against all this, as we have seen, is raised the cry of the letter killing, of the spirit alone mattering, of the cardinal need for flexibility. Certainly there must be liberty of spirit, but it must denote a freedom *in* rule and *under* rule, and not a freedom *from* rule.

Any anti-reformer who is prepared calmly and carefully to read the hundred and eighteenth psalm should be able to see by the time he has finished the exercise what the man is driving at who pledges himself to the stricter view. "That my ways may be directed to keep thy justifications." It is not just fussiness over details that makes the psalmist call out to the Lord: "I have been delighted in the way of thy testimonies as in all riches; I will meditate on thy commandments, and will consider thy ways." Nor is the psalmist responding to any mere aesthetic appeal. The law means sacrifice as well as security in the love of God. The psalmist prays that the love of God's justifications may come between the soul and vanity, may turn his sight away from earthly things and fix it upon the things of heaven. In this can be found the whole purpose of monastic legislation: it is the means designed to wean the soul from the world and develop the powers, natural and supernatural, in a Godward direction.

If a monastery has not turned its back upon the vanity of the world, it is not justifying its existence and has no right to expect vocations. In the same way, if a monk has not turned his back upon the vanity of the world, he is a dead weight upon the community and has no right to expect the graces of his state. This argument would seem to require no proof; it is assumed in the terms of the monastic purpose. In spite of this it is commonly said in praise of a monastery that it does not take things too seriously; of a monk it is sometimes said to his credit that he mixes on equal terms with men of the world. What is this all about? When it is an undoubted fact that a community is more often recommended for its joviality than for its regularity, one begins to wonder whether St. Benedict's intention has ever been seriously examined. In his Rule St. Benedict if anything discourages the spirit of hilarity,[2] yet it is the hilarious communities that make a name for themselves in the world outside. St. Benedict makes a great point of silence, punctuality, poverty, enclosure; but it is the more broadminded communities that find favour with the majority of laymen. The truth of it is that the

[2] See ch. 4, fifty-fourth and fifty-fifth instrument of good works; also ch. 7, tenth and eleventh degree of humility.

worldly, whether outside or inside the cloister, do not like monks to be either too reformed or too unreformed: they like them to be as they themselves are. The reformed are too much of a reproach to their consciences; the deliberately lax are anomalous. It is always easier to get on with one's own kind. But of course the whole point is that the monk is not of the same kind as the man of the world. The whole point of the monastic separation is that a quite different, and now a supernatural, kind has been substituted. The call is to a complete break, a break from the views and standards and aims that were before. It is the vocation of Abram over again: "Come out from thy country and from thy kindred and from thy father's house, and come into the land which I will show thee."[3] To make the geographical change while in mind remaining a man of Ur or Haran is to defeat the main purpose of the grace.

Those who have nice things to say only of those monasteries where high spirits prevail would do well to examine the case for strictness in regard to silence and poverty. Gaiety in a community *may* be a good sign, but on the other hand it may have nothing supernatural about it. It may be on exactly the same level as what you would find in the holiday season at a youth hostel.

One reason why silence and poverty are at least as sure an indication of the monastery's authentic spirit

[3] Gen. 12; 1.

as hilarity—indeed, if our argument has been accepted, a surer indication—is that silence points to reverence for the presence of God and poverty points to sacrifice. Hilarity may point, in a roundabout way, to fraternal charity, but it has to make very sure of this or it may justly be taken for dissipation and indifference to the relevant degrees of humility as laid down by St. Benedict. If St. Benedict's Rule is to be made the touchstone of these issues—and it is the thesis of this chapter and of this book that it can be made the touchstone of every monastic issue, controversial or other—then the best witness to a true community spirit is a respect for those things which the idealistic join a community to find. A man does not join a community for companionship: he can find that in the world. It is not the community recreations that influence him in making the final decision. He asks admission to the community because he hopes to find among the brethren those qualities which will help him in his pursuit of perfection, in his progress towards union with God. He hopes to find in the monastery that silence which will induce him to pray, and which will increasingly become to him the environment in which all his works are performed. He hopes to find that standard of poverty which will make of him demands which, left to himself, he is unable to impose. He hopes to find rules relating to enclosure, timetable, obedience and the common life which will prove to be the discipline which his soul needs, which will detach him from his own will and train his whole effort upon God. That is why he comes into the monastery, and it is on this that his development in God's service may reasonably be estimated.

4

Development
According to Prayer

THE MONK'S PROGRESS in perfection is his progress in
prayer. His monastic vocation is directed primarily
towards prayer, and it is prayer that gives to whatever
else he does the value by which his perfection will be
judged. By prayer a monk comes to enter more fully
into the life of Christ, and by prayer the life of Christ
comes to enter more fully into him. The monk's perfection is accordingly Christ's achievement rather than
the monk's; it is the work of grace responded to in
prayer rather than in pursuit of an object which
is sanctity. There is a difference between seeing development as increasing submission to the influence of the
Holy Spirit and seeing it as fidelity to a career which
happens to have holiness as its goal. In the one case
monastic perfection is looked upon in terms of pleasing God, and as a means; in the other it is proposed in
terms of realizing an ambition, and therefore as an end
in itself. For the soul's conception of sanctity to be
raised to the strictly supernatural level—as for the conception of monasticism to be raised to the strictly super-

natural level—there is need for prayer. The soul of prayer, increasingly enlightened by grace, comes to see the implications of sanctity and monasticism from God's angle rather than from man's. Sanctity fits in as part of God's design; monasticism fits in as part of God's design. The end of it all, like the beginning of it all, is God himself. He alone is the consummation, as he alone is the inspiration. *Alpha* and *omega*: the foundations on which monasteries are built.

In the foregoing chapter we have seen how monastic perfection will show itself in monastic observance; we come now to see how this perfection is dependent upon, and measured by, fidelity to prayer. But in working from the outward to the inward we still have to draw more upon the evidence of sense than upon the evidence of spirit. While it is the interior life that matters more than the exterior, it is the exterior tests that reveal the spirit of the interior. Neither the human reason which tries to analyse the spiritual life, nor the human emotions which try to get mixed up in it, can give a satisfactory account of how the soul is responding to the operation of grace. Though the process can never, in the nature of the case, be fully explained, it can at least be verified. The use of outward signs and symbols is not applied in the hope of communicating the incommunicable: they are merely bearing witness to the authenticity of the act. Because he is part natural and part supernatural, man has to be judged on his natural and on his supernatural performance. The mistake is to judge the two separately instead of taking man as a unity and letting the one side of him prove the other. The natural proclaims and disposes for the supernatural; the supernatural lifts up the natural and sanctifies it. So much for the principle; from the point of view of estimating the success of its application it is necessarily the natural and the external which provide the findings.

Assuming that the thesis as so far expressed is accepted, and that the monastic life is the channel by which the soul moves towards union with God in perfect charity, the monk's immediate business is to acquire the habit of living as far as possible in God's presence. The monk tries to perform all his works in the element which his set times of prayer create. The foreground of his prayer activity becomes the background of his activity outside the hours of prayer. The frame of monasticism is designed precisely to promote this development, which it serves at the same time to reflect. The Rule, the vows, the observance: these things begin by helping the soul to pray and end by revealing new manifestations of the soul's prayer. The structure looks inwards at recollection, and recollection lights up the structure. There is no development without recollection, and there is no recollection without development.

Recollection, then, is not only the first practice which

the soul will try to learn on entering religion but is also the final grace to which the soul may justly aspire. In one form it marks the initiation, and in another the consummation. So it is that whatever furthers recollection can be taken as a means willed by God for the soul's sanctification—provided always that obedience and charity give their sanction—and whatever hinders it must call for correction. Development according to prayer is not a different kind of development from that which is according to rule or according to charity; it is simply the deepening of recollection. Understood in its monastic context it is a perfection which is both safeguarded and expressed in specifically monastic terms. While spiritual progress conforms to the recognized pattern—developing through the purgative to the illuminative and unitive states—a monastic vocation supposes standards and sanctions which are different from those applied by souls leading the interior life in the world.

Looking first at the obstacles to prayer and recollection before examining the factors which influence positively towards God, we can note that the hindrances arise out of either an unquiet mind, an unquiet heart, or an unquiet sense. Sometimes they arise out of all three. The classification is very rough, and there are times when the soul is genuinely unable to judge the source of the disturbance, but in trying to make sure of the elusive quality of prayerful calm we have to take whatever helps we can get.

64

The obstacles which come about because of an unquiet mind are not restricted to the field of the intellect.
Intellectual doubts may rob the mind of the tranquillity required for interior prayer, but the passions can
cause almost as much agitation in the mind as they can
in the heart and in the senses. If the exercise is to
mount to God on the unimpeded impulse of grace, the
mind must be raised not only above doubt and speculation but also above worry, fear, preoccupation about
work, the desire to know that all is going well in the
spiritual life, over-eagerness and a too superficial joy.
To this list St. Bernard would add excessive remorse
and the humility which is self-regarding instead of related to the humility of Christ. In the measure that the
mind is concerned with its own affairs, even if these
affairs are holy, the movement of prayer is delayed.
That is why the virtue of absolute trust in God is so
much insisted upon by the saints and mystical writers.
Even the necessities, let alone those things that are not
necessary, must be transcended in the act of trust which
is prayer. At the same time it must be remembered
that matters of pressing business will inevitably come
before the mind during prayer: the very act of disen-
gaging attention from many objects disposes for the
intrusion of one particular object. Though the one
particular object is meant to be God, the emergency
of the moment may well force itself for the time being
into the space which the soul has tried to leave free for

him. Though there is no avoiding this on occasion, the soul must guard against the habit, more or less conscious, of trying to settle practical problems while pretending to pray.

Obstacles which result from an unquiet heart are no less distracting to prayer. Indeed they are probably more distracting. Thus the effect of unregulated affection, romantic daydreaming, jealousy, sentimental regret and the movements of memory in general, excitement, ambition and a too great freedom of imagination —the whole range, in other words, of the emotional faculties—cannot but be harmful to true prayer. Nevertheless it must again be remembered that much of all this is inescapable, and that only the indulgence of these distracting impulses is culpable. The heart, like the mind, is a restless organ, and perhaps never more so than when setting itself to desire only God. When God does not make his presence felt to the soul, other attractions are found to crowd in. Since the heart cannot picture God whom it loves, how can it help picturing in prayer those whom it also loves and whom it *can* picture? But though the affections remain, neither still nor neutral, there is still the obligation of trying to train its activity during prayer exclusively towards God. All too easily we can waft our way through half an hour of mental prayer, and through much longer periods of time which might be spent in recollection, or in an enterprise which strives to combine human and divine love

66

and which we vaguely call charity. Such an exercise may possibly produce good resolutions and give us a new point of view, but it is not strictly an act of worship. For true prayer to rise up from the heart there must be stillness in the heart. By stirring the emotions, even when this is done from the best of motives, we are liable to make one of two mistakes: either we stir the wrong emotions for the particular work in hand, or we stir the right emotions but in such a way that the pleasure which we get out of the undertaking is greater than the praise which is given to God. The Father is to be worshipped in spirit and in truth, not in a bubbling emotion which looks more to the gratification of self than to the glory of God.

The third group of obstacles, those which come from a lack of tranquillity in the senses, can be dealt with very briefly. It is obvious that physical restlessness, curiosity, the desire to hear and see what is going on during prayer, deliberate interruptions—indeed any unnecessary outward activity which experience has shown to be inconsistent with recollection—must lessen the soul's awareness of the presence of God. The set exercise of prayer, whether mental or liturgical, is not like that of eating, which can be performed while reading a book, nor yet like that of driving a car, which can be managed while listening to a broadcast; the specific act of prayer, as distinct now from the habit of recollection, is an exclusive act. This does not mean that a man must spend his time of prayer in one position and with his eyes shut. Certainly in the case of liturgical prayer the senses are actively engaged, and even in the case of mental prayer it is sometimes a good thing to walk about. What it means is that the bodily powers must be made to co-operate with the action of prayer, and not be allowed to work away from it. The movement must be all in one direction with no diversionary interest. In the prayer effort there must be co-ordination of body, heart, and head. Even then there will be distractions, but not of the kind that can do much harm.

Turning now to the positive side of the question, we can see at once that among the influences which give impulse to prayer the most effective are reading, silence, solitude, manual labour, and the cultivation of the particular control which, on the lines of the above summary, is found to be weak. Other factors which have their bearing upon the life of prayer are listening to spiritual conferences, preparing and preaching sermons which relate to contemplation, studying and writing about dogmatic and mystical theology and the Scriptures, receiving and giving spiritual direction. Since our main concern is with monastic spirituality, it is the first group of influences which will be considered here.

For prayer of any kind, but for the prayer of the monk especially, silence is not only a safeguard but a necessity. Monasteries are meant to be enclaves of silence in a society which has long lost the faculty of keeping quiet comfortably. Monasticism does not try to keep pace with civilization either in noise or in anything else. Monasticism has a quite different idea about the use of sound and about silence. In the world men tend to think out loud, are conditioned to noise, take speech to be the normal and constant accompaniment to life. In the monastery men think silently, are conditioned to stillness, and look upon speech simply as a means either of conveying information or of sounding the praises of God. "Not to speak useless words" is the fifty-fourth instrument of good works in St. Benedict's fourth chapter. St. Benedict underlines the same doctrine in the sixth chapter where he says that "because of the importance of silence let permission to speak be seldom given." The ninth degree of humility, from the seventh and most significant chapter in the holy Rule, demands "that a monk restrain his tongue from speaking, keeping silence until he is questioned."

It has been objected that if everyone in the monastery observed this rule of not speaking unless spoken to, there would be no talking at all. Exactly. Apart from necessary business, which had to be conducted at convenient times, *horis competentibus*,[1] and whatever occasions were allowed by obedience, silence was the general rule throughout the day and throughout the monastery. Monks should practise silence at all times,

[1] Ch. 31.

omni tempore silentium debent studere monachi.[2]
There is no mention in the holy Rule of private conversations being allowed between monk and monk, nor do we hear of regular community recreations as we know them today.

Those who consider that modern conditions and needs would warrant the rejection of St. Benedict's ideal of silence may have much to justify their view. We are not here concerned with the excuses which let us out of following the ideal; we are concerned with the ideal itself, and with its bearing upon the question of prayer. It is indisputable that, if the mind is to remain recollected, the power of speech must be used sparingly. "If the lips are to be opened," says the seventeenth-century authority, Dom Haeften, commenting on the degrees of humility, "it must be with the key of the mind." Unless the mind is conditioned to silence, *taciturnitatem habens*,[3] the lips will be opened to no purpose.

Thus the value of what a monk says will depend upon the silence from which he says it. If he speaks from the silence of recollection, his words will be worth listening to; if he speaks from a distracted or wasted silence, his words will be empty. Silence is a good which is easily frittered away; few goods are so lightly broken. The degree to which silence is observed by a monk

[2] Ch. 42.
[3] Ch. 7.

is the degree to which prayer is valued by that monk. The degree to which silence is observed in a monastery is the degree to which prayer is valued in that monastery.

Those who imagine that the life of prayer can be developed irrespective of the spirit and discipline of silence might as well talk of developing a feeling for the Mass irrespective of the words and ceremonial of the missal. Silence is not the same as prayer, any more than ceremonial is the same as sacrifice, but just as Christ's sacrificial act is enshrined in liturgical forms, so silence enshrines the act of prayer.

Ranking close to silence in its influence upon prayer is monastic solitude. Since the place of solitude in Benedictine spirituality will be considered in the second half of this book, only the briefest treatment of the subject will be given here. As an immediate factor in the soul's relationship with God, solitude must be accounted for together with silence and reading in the group of formative influences; as the background to monastic activity, and therefore in a wider frame of reference, it can be dealt with more fully later on.

Just as a monk's talk takes its character from his silence, so a monk's manner, movements, and general way of behaving will reflect the use which the monk makes of the hours when he is alone. In the *Compendium Asceseos Benedictinae,* the second in the list of means by which habitual recollection is acquired and maintained is *custodia cellae.* The text goes on: *e qua nonnisi casu necessitatis, utilitatis, aut charitatis causa, animo ad Deum elevato prodeundum; et quidem auribus et oculis custoditis, ne Deus vel minimum offendatur.*[4] If this should appear to us rigorist, we should remind ourselves that it is in the classical Benedictine tradition. It is simply a particular application of St. Benedict's general principles as expressed especially in chapters seven, forty-two, and sixty-six.

The problem for the monk is not only that of preserving for himself a measure of physical solitude, but also that of developing a spiritual solitude out of whatever physical solitude he is able to secure. It is no good being alone for the sake of being alone. If isolation is not a disposition for something else, it might just as well be abandoned for something else. The isolation which monasticism tries to guarantee for its followers is full of purpose: it is planned as the setting for prayer. Solitude is not the establishment of loneliness but the open avenue of God's approach. Solitude does not stop short at hedging the soul about in the attempt to keep away distractions and interruptions; it goes on to the work of building up a cell of prayer. Solitude is meant

[4] "Not to leave it except for reasons of necessity, utility, charity, but to keep there the mind directed towards God, so that by watchfulness over sight and hearing, no offense may be given to God."—Poson, 1852, p. 12.

to generate prayerfulness. Solitude, rightly handled, can become charged with the presence of God. Understood in this sense, solitude is not only an opportunity but a grace. Like all graces it carries with it the grace of being further developed.

Consequently a man who has no love for being alone, who is by nature gregarious, can cultivate a true feeling for solitude. It will be grace that gives him the attraction in the first place, and grace again that gives him perseverance in its practice. The distinction should perhaps be noted here between the feeling *for* solitude and the feeling *of* it. If the solitude is to be fruitful, the attraction must be according to grace and not simply according to nature. To have the feeling of being withdrawn from the world is at best a variable emotion, which may or may not deepen the soul's recollection. To have the desire of being alone for God alone—and to see God's love through the solitude, and to desire God's love beyond the love of solitude—is the authentic quality, and cannot but deepen the soul's recollection.

It is only in solitude, prayer, and silence that a man comes to see below the surface of things and to find his true self. While it is undeniable that solitude reluctantly accepted has the effect of reducing a man's spiritual vigour, causing him to drag his soul along after him in a state of smouldering despair, the right use of both solitude and the means to attain it brings calm, detachment, and happiness. Just as fidelity to St. Benedict's injunction about keeping silence until spoken to establishes a deep peace in the soul and helps the activity of prayer, so fidelity to the ideal of solitude does the same. The monk who cherishes his isolation to the extent of leaving the enclosure only when obedience and charity combine to make it a duty, and who writes only such letters as are strictly necessary (here again *taciturnitatem habens usque ad interrogationem,* keeping silence until questioned), finds himself not only freed of much distraction but positively founded in tranquillity. In excluding news, gossip, sight and sound of the outside world from his range of interest he may lay himself open to the charge of narrowness, but if he is imposing these restrictions upon himself for the love of God and on the impulse of grace he will be no loser. Far from having a narrowing effect, the resolve will in fact widen his horizon, enabling him to see the things of God *as* the things of God, and the things of man in their right relation.

"Have nothing to do with crowds," says St. Bernard, "nothing to do with the masses of mankind. Forget also your own people and your father's house; so shall the King have pleasure in your beauty. Remain alone, consecrated soul, so as to preserve yourself for him alone whom you have chosen for yourself from among all others. Avoid appearing in public, shun even those who dwell in the house with you, withdraw yourself from friends and intimates. Do you not know that you have a Bridegroom who is diffident, who is not willing to honour you when others are present? Withdraw yourself therefore; I do not mean in body so much as in mind, in intention, in devotion, and in spirit. For the Lord Christ . . . would wear away the night alone in prayer, withdrawing himself not only from the crowds which followed him but also from the company of his disciples and familiar friends."[5]

Fidelity to solitude and fidelity to observance go together. When St. Augustine said that "the written law is our firmament" he might equally have said that solitude is for the monk his firmament. If monastic life is lived under the sky of the holy Rule, open to what is written in the heavens for our particular sanctification as monks, then the element in which that life is led is solitude. We work in it and from it; it covers us all the time.

As a rider, though not as an afterthought, comes the question of manual labour. If the approach to monasticism was at one time by way of the fields, it can hardly be said to be so today. Certainly there are many monasteries, Benedictine as well as Cistercian, where manual labour is still, as it was in St. Benedict's time, the normal work of the monks. There are signs, furthermore, which suggest that the present century may yet

[5] *Sermons on the Canticle*, 40.

see among Benedictines a widespread return to the kind of working day which is outlined by St. Benedict in his forty-eighth chapter. Interesting as it would be to develop this speculation, our concern with manual labour is more immediately in connection with prayer than with controversy and possible points of reform.

The degree to which prayer is helped by manual labour is the degree to which it is performed in silence and solitude. Solitude without labour can be conducive towards recollection, but labour without solitude can scarcely be regarded as so effective an influence. The manual labour which is done in common will also, if it is to be a labour of the spirit as well as of the body, have to be done in silence and away from the crowd. It is not the presence of other human beings that lessens the value of manual labour as an exercise of the spirit but the absence of recollection. Recollection can be lost or found in either company or solitude, but it is not likely to be practised where there is conversation.

Given silence and a measure of isolation, there is hardly any physical work which may not be performed in a state of recollection. While grace is needed for the exercise, it is a grace which the soul can count upon without presumption. Obviously a greater effort of concentration will be required, and longer practice, to preserve an awareness of God's presence when engaged in carpentry than when hoeing and digging and picking fruit, but it would be a mistake to imagine that prayer need be attempted only when the work is more or less mechanical. Even in those works which demand great accuracy and quick decisions it should be possible to supply for sustained recollection with the prayer of intermittent ejaculation. Certainly the saints seem to have praised God while working with their hands, whether the particular job called for precision or merely repetitive action, and we are not expected to attribute the whole of this to grace alone. What happens in the case of a saint is surely that he sets himself to acquire the habit, which, because grace is all along the line more faithfully responded to, is finally possessed in greater perfection. By responding to the impulse which urges us to recollection during our manual labour we can accordingly come by God's grace not only to the prolonged awareness which we want but also to an appreciation of manual labour as one of the most powerful forces in the direction of our monastic vocation.

In his encyclical letter on St. Benedict, and again in his sermon on the occasion of St. Benedict's centenary, Pope Pius XII stresses in his outline of the monastic ideal the part played by manual labour. Where others have been inclined to see it in its negative function— as subduing the flesh, preventing idleness, atoning for sin, humbling the mind and body, imposing a discipline which wears down the man's natural instability— the Pope refers to the sanctifying power of manual

77

labour, and to the lessons which it preaches.[6] Men in the world are expected to learn, from the example set by monks, about the dignity of toiling with the hands and about elemental truths which our mechanical and technical civilization is in danger of overlooking.

"It is difficult to say," writes Cassian about the monks with whom he had trained in the East, "whether it is in order to meditate better that they occupy themselves unceasingly in manual work, or whether it is by this constancy in toil that they acquire such devotion, knowledge, and light."[7]

The strength which is brought to prayer by reading and study has been left for consideration to the last because, in a way which silence, solitude, and manual labour are not, the exercise of St. Benedict's *lectio divina* is almost a part of prayer itself. Certainly the ancients viewed it as such, making it the first of the degrees of prayer which culminate in union: *lectio, cogitatio, studium, meditatio, oratio, contemplatio.* Though it is true that systematized prayer is a comparatively modern development, it is not altogether true to say that the early monks knew no method. They were clear enough about an ascending scale of spiritual exercises by which the soul might be expected to mount to

[6] *Fulgens radiatur,* March 21, 1947, and also in the sermon preached on September 18 of the same year.
[7] *Institutions,* bk. 2; ch. 14.

God. "So going in," they could have quoted from the book of Esther, "she passed through all the doors in order, and stood before the king where he sat."[8] There is order without the hampering restrictions of system. "Contemplation without preparation or without rules," says St. Gregory Nazianzen, "leads to nothing but illusion."[9] For prayer there has to be order, and for order there has to be a plan. The plan, the order, and to a certain extent the prayer itself, are conditioned by the right use of reading.

Since St. Bernard has been taken as our authority in interpreting St. Benedict's mind, he can be quoted here at some length in confirmation of what has been noted above. "Reading is to be regarded as a foundation. Having laid this foundation with the proper material, reading draws on the soul to meditation. Meditation in its turn leads the mind to enquire into what must be sought, and almost like digging up a treasure sends the soul to search in prayer. Then prayer, lifting itself with all its powers to the Lord, implores this most desirable treasure which is the good of contemplation. The Saviour tells us: 'Seek and you shall find; knock and it shall be opened to you. Seek by reading, and you will find by meditation. Knock on the door by sincere prayer, and it will be opened to you by contemplation. Reading is the earnest searching of the Scriptures with

[8] 15; 9.
[9] *In S. Lumina,* ch. 8.

the whole intent of the soul. Meditation is the studious action of the mind investigating the knowledge of hidden truth under the leadership of reason. Prayer is the devoted direction of the intellect to God for the removal of evils and the acquisition of virtue. Contemplation is the elevation of the soul, suspended in God, drinking in the joys of eternal sweetness.''[10]

A monk's reading should accordingly be related rather to his prayer than to any of his other activities. To make use of *lectio divina* to store up preaching material may be praiseworthy enough, but the primary purpose of the exercise is not served. St. Benedict's purpose in setting aside a large part of each day for it is to make of spiritual reading a direct means of personal spiritual advancement in the soul's personal relationship with God. If prayer is not supposed to be used—except indirectly by providing the light and purity of intention—as preparation for what is to be spoken and written, so neither is reading. Reading does a work in its own right—a right that is given to it by prayer.

Added to the questions of how and why to read, there is the question of what to read. We have seen that the right way to read is recollectively ("Even while reading," says Sulpicius Severus of St. Martin, "he never relaxed his mind from prayer"),[11] and that the

[10] *Scala Claustralium: sive tractatus de modo orandi,* 1; 2.
[11] *Vita,* ch. 26.

80

reason for it is spiritual nourishment ("Reading is a food for the soul," says Dom Mabillon, "and unless you repeatedly strengthen it with this food, the soul will be weak and indisposed for all its function");[12] we must now consider the choice of books. The literature most immediately profitable to the soul is clearly the literature of the Bible. If the taste for biblical study and reading is not there, it can be acquired; if it is there, it can be developed. The desert monks had practically no reading apart from the Old and New Testaments, and it is from Egypt, Palestine, and Syria that St. Benedict inherits his tradition. In the holy Rule there are ninety-five Old Testament references; the New Testament is quoted directly or indirectly one hundred and four times. In his twenty-eighth chapter St. Benedict reveals in the telling expression *medicamina Scripturarum divinarum* his attitude towards the study of God's word. The Bible is for him health-bringing, therapeutic. Read but the word and our souls shall be healed. The same idea is found in St. Ambrose, who says: "But you when you read the Gospel must know as a wise man what is read. Let the brightness of eternal wisdom enlighten you. These are words which you read, but they purify. They give light; they give strength."

It is significant, too, that of the ninety-five Old Testament references in the Rule, fifty-nine are from

[12] *De monasticorum studiorum ratione ad juniores monachos.*

the psalms. The psalms are so often quoted by St.
Bernard, whose style in any case is vividly scriptural,
that it is sometimes difficult to tell where the psalmist
leaves off and the saint goes on. Dom Mabillon in his
Tractatus de studiis monasticis makes especial mention
of the psalter, which he singles out for the attention of
the younger brethren: "All the studies of religious must
tend powerfully towards, and aim directly at, the Scriptures. The special concern of these studies should be
the understanding of the psalms, which religious con-
stantly recite, and the reading and meditation of the
gospels and epistles, which embrace the very summit
of Christian doctrine."

The monk whose reading is the inspired word of
God comes close to the Word himself who imparts his
Spirit through the written text. Approaching the Scriptures for the moral and mystical doctrine that can be
learned from them, a soul is able to cut through the
tangle of critical apparatus which would separate the
rationalist from their true value. Like Mary who pon-
dered the actions and spoken words of Christ, the
soul comes increasingly to dwell upon the mysteries
of the revealed word. *Mirabilia testimonia tua; ideo
scrutata est ea anima mea ... praevenerunt oculi mei ad
te diluculo ut meditarer eloquia tua.*[13] The "testi-

[13] "Thy testimonies are wonderful; therefore my soul hath
sought them . . . my eyes to thee have prevented the dawn,
that I might meditate on thy words."—Psalm 118; 129, 148.

monies" of God are seen to be increasingly marvellous as we study them: we are encouraged to search after them more and more. Meditating upon God's words becomes our desire. *In lege ejus meditabitur die ac nocte; et erit tamquam lignum quod plantatum est secus decursus aquarum, quod fructum suum dabit in tempore suo.*[14] The exercise brings security in faith and hope; its reward is peace of mind and fruitfulness in labour.

Next after the Scriptures, St. Benedict would put as reading material for his monks the works of the Fathers. These, he says in his final chapter, are "manifestly devoted to teaching us the straight road to our Creator." He follows his recommendations about scriptural and patristic reading by advising the *Conferences* and *Institutes* of Cassian, the *Lives of the Fathers,* and the *Rule of St. Basil.* The list is not meant to be exhaustive but directive: it indicates the lines along which a monk's literary taste should develop. With such a ground-plan of reading the monk of today would not find himself starved of either spiritual or intellectual interest, but because few modern monks will be persuaded of this it is only fair to admit that any work by an approved Catholic authority, provided its purpose is spiritual and

[14] "Upon his law he shall meditate day and night; he shall be like a tree that is planted near running waters, which shall bring forth its fruit in due season."—Psalm 1; 2, 3.

not polemical or purely speculative, may be taken to come within St. Benedict's designation *lectio divina*.

To sum up this chapter, then, it may be said that progress in monastic life is progress in prayer, and that this is judged mainly by the soul's readiness to go on with it, to follow the counsels regarding it, and to apply the measures which safeguard it. It may be said further that there is no true monastic prayer, whatever the devotion to the external forms of the liturgy, where silence, solitude, reading and work are neglected. Prayer moreover is here to be thought of neither exclusively as the set exercise nor exclusively as recollection but rather as the combined activity which results in a deepening and extending of faith. From the set period of prayer during which the soul knows experimentally the nothingness of earthly things, a certain confused knowledge of supernatural values is carried into the rest of the day. Actual awareness, when the soul gets up from prayer and goes on to the next duty, tends to evaporate. But actual awareness is not the qualifying factor. By translating the wisdom learned in prayer into everyday terms the soul comes to live in a more or less habitual state of supernatural appreciation. While not always conscious of God's presence, the soul reveals in the response which is given to the changing stimuli of outward events a conviction born of light in prayer that the material world is dust and ashes and that the spiritual world is all.

Of this prayer—since it is a grace, and graces defy measurement—there can be no direct test. All that can be tested, and that not very profitably, is the soul's fidelity to it. In effect, does the impression of truth, the apprehension of God's divine purpose, remain fixed at the back of the mind in times of excitement, anxiety, over-work, exasperation and other nervous or emotional tension? "The soul raises itself in prayer," says Cassian, "according to the degree of its purity. The more it withdraws from the sight of material and terrestrial things, the more is it purified and is given to see Jesus Christ interiorly . . . they alone can contemplate his divinity with a most pure eye who turn away from base and earthly thoughts and works to mount with him the high mountain of solitude, where they contemplate by the light of their faith the glory of his face."[15]

From the same authority a further passage may be quoted which bears out the theme not only of the present chapter but of the whole of this book. If Cassian's postulate is accepted, then the monastic points at issue must cease to be points of monastic dispute. "The whole scope of monastic life," says the master to whom St. Benedict looked more than to any other in the monastic field, "and its highest perfection con-

[15] *Conferences,* 10; 6.

85

sist in a constant and uninterrupted perseverance in prayer, and in preserving, so far as human frailty will permit, peace of soul and purity of heart. To attain this most precious good, all the efforts of our body and all the aspirations of our mind should be directed. And there are between these two things, namely prayer and perfection, close and necessary relations. The whole edifice of the virtues is raised only to attain the perfection of prayer, and if it is not crowned with prayer, which unites and binds all the parts together, it will neither be solid nor lasting."[16] If this leaves no doubt as to what monasteries are for, it leaves even less as to the first work of the individual monk. It is on this work that he, as also his monastery, will be judged.

[16] *Ibid.*, 9; 2.

5

Deviations
to be Denied

GOD'S GRACE is such that it is rare for a monk to decide upon altering the course which he had set for himself at the beginning of his religious life. What more often happens is that by giving a false emphasis to one or other aspect of his vocation he arrives at a state of indifference about the course which he is really supposed to be following. He may even lose his sense of direction altogether. A man does not as a rule become clumsy in the handling of one lot of principles unless he becomes preoccupied in handling another. Energy which is diverted to something good in itself, but which is not the appropriate good proposed by the monastic life, is energy for the most part wasted. In certain circumstances such an activity may even do positive harm. Energy, again, which is directed towards the true monastic aim, but which is wrongly expended, is also wasteful and possibly harmful. It is a mistake to imagine that the main obstacle to monastic perfection is lack of effort; more often it is over-effort which is misapplied. Laziness may well be a contributing factor in monastic failure—in the sense that want of interest and occupation leads to a search for self-expression which may have unfortunate consequences—but it is seldom the cause. The significant cause, as also the significant consequence, is a combination of ambition, obstinacy, pride.

As in the case of religion in general, about which it is a commonplace to observe that exaggeration of a doctrine does no service to truth but in fact does harm to it, so in the case of monasticism the true service of God may suffer untold harm by the toleration of a mania. Whether it happens to be a monastic or a non-monastic mania, the monk must have none of it. Monks are meant to be balanced souls, secure upon the balance of truth. Monasteries are not made for maniacs, fanatics, eccentrics. Monasteries make room for individualists, do their best to correct the self-opinionated, but cannot be expected to show sympathy for extravagant enthusiasts who live on singularity and attention. Champions of an exhibitionist monasticism manage sometimes to get admitted to monasteries, but they do not flourish there. They find themselves in the end damaging precisely the cause to which they have pledged themselves.

The true reformer is of a different quality. For him it is a cardinal principle to exert an even pressure along the whole front. In order to meet a particular abuse or neglect, the true reformer may judge it necessary to single out a particular doctrine and to take steps, as though nothing else mattered, to see that it is properly understood. But since the holy Rule hangs together as a single whole, and since monasticism is a balanced ideal, it is the harmony of the life, rather than any one interpretation of it, that has to be aimed at. The monastic vocation, like charity itself, is a harmony. *Ordinavit in me charitatem.*[1] He has ordered in me also the monastic virtues and the monastic purposes.

Occasions of giving stress to a side-issue of monasticism at the expense of the monastic issue itself are too many to enumerate. A man can make a fad of almost any authentic conception or cause. None of St. Benedict's ideals is proof against anomaly, disproportion, caricature. Monks can make a fetish of the *opus Dei* and sacrifice prayer to performance, can press the need of manual labour to the detriment of necessary theological study, can so canonize the common life as not to allow themselves the solitude which monasticism demands. You get aberrations of one sort or another in almost every community. Nor is the phenomenon confined to religious communities; people living in the world can, every bit as easily as those living in monasteries, allow their minds to follow a single track. Looking neither to right nor left, and congratulating ourselves upon our single-mindedness, we pursue our

[1] Cant. 2; 4.

89

particular foibles to the disadvantage of our souls and to the disedification of our fellows.

The most common monastic deviation, and the one which is most pounced upon by our critics outside, is that which subordinates religion to routine. A monk can set himself such a high standard of punctuality, silence, poverty, and enclosure as to overlook the claims of Christian charity. To the perfectionist—and the monk is supposed to be a perfectionist in the principal activity of his life—there is always a drawback in exercises which of their nature are both repetitious and capable of almost indefinite exactitude. Religious have more reason than any to remind themselves that the mind must be informed by charity before its acts are regulated by habit. We are always in danger of serving observance when it is observance that should be serving us—in the further work of serving God. The horarium which is designed to regulate our day, training us in detachment, obedience, self-discipline, is not meant to give the last word to our response to grace. We do not follow the timetable today merely for the sake of following the same timetable tomorrow.

Where the outward is so closely interlocked with the inward, and where both outward and inward are based upon the service of God, the practical test is simply "to what am I ministering?" Am I being punctual in the name of punctuality or for the glory of God? Am I practising poverty in the name of economy or because

Christ chose to be poor? Am I stopping within the enclosure because there happen to be boundaries to the monastic property and it is nice to feel that I never step outside them, or because I allow my observance of enclosure to serve St. Benedict's purpose of furthering the life of prayer?

Always in this matter of false emphasis the most usual occasion is, as it was in our Lord's time in the case of the Jewish priesthood with their temple worship, the liturgy. The old Benedictine formula which proudly claims that monks are *propter chorum fundati* can give rise to some unfortunate misconceptions. Not only can elaborate liturgical worship be no more than a front, but, such is the irony which attends man's deviations, it can come to be its own enemy. Too great an insistence on detail, by inducing weariness and distaste, reduces the perfection of its actual rendering. Without even being aware of the implied cynicism, a monk can come to look upon himself as privileged when allowed to be absent from choir. Once the system known as "half-choirs" is taken to be a reward and not an anomaly, St. Benedict's *nihil operi Dei praeponatur* is rendered meaningless. In liturgical matters, as in so many others, it is nearly always the meticulous and the forced that is the obstacle to true development. If the liturgy means worship, the ideal must mean evenness, tranquillity, strength. The ideal is the prayer of Christ, and if obedience dispenses him from taking his public part in this prayer the monk submits himself in all humility and does not think of himself as privileged.

Thus while the level of monastic orthodoxy may be preserved intact, it is possible for the basic principles of monasticism to fall apart. Again and again in history it can be seen how the liturgy, which officially enthrones these monastic principles, has tended to become largely a matter of ritualism to be enjoyed aesthetically by those who have a taste for such things, and to be evaded by those who have not.

Almost as deceptive a deviation is the fallacy of constant work, hard work, work for the good of others. Every excellence casts a shadow, and we can work ourselves to death in the darkness which lies behind the excellence of service, toil, zeal for the well-being of our neighbour. Work which is begun in the spirit must be maintained in the spirit; otherwise it will end in the factory or the social service centre. Since they have so close a bearing upon the life itself, these two aspects of monastic work—the one relating to production, the other to the apostolate—will have to be treated separately.

When the monk sees himself as serving output and industry instead of serving God he will know that he must slow down and begin again. A man is meant to be the master of his labour, not its slave. The work of a man's hands is to be understood in terms of the man and of God, not in terms of more and more work. If either quantitative production, technical efficiency, or economic security were the first concern of monasticism, then the monk would have every reason to strain his powers to the utmost in the effort to yield results. But outward returns are of secondary interest to monasticism, and are furthermore no very sure guide to its spirit. Outward returns can possess a fascination for certain types of mind, and in the monastic life no less than in the world of business the lure of figures is considerable.

Even where there is no desire to seek consolation in statistics there is often a purely natural desire to seek consolation in work itself. It becomes a drug, an escape. The man can become so caught up in the machine that he begins to drop the monastery which gives meaning to the machine. Work is so easy to justify; the motives behind it so difficult to detect. The only test must lie, as always, in its effects. The effects will show up eventually in the monk's prayer, in his standards of observance, in the clarity with which the monastic ideal presents itself. When private interpretations are made, substituting one form of duty for another and canonizing the industrious before all other, it is then high time to investigate the nature of the energy and to re-direct it towards God.

Deviated monastic labour, as in the case of deviated liturgical activity, defeats itself in the long run. By this is meant not only that the human engine, when raced beyond a certain length of time, becomes exhausted; it means also that exhaustion inevitably follows the expenditure of effort that is misdirected. The necessary vitality may be present, but because it has attached itself to the wrong dynamo it splutters and dies out before its time. The motor force, which in the activities of monasticism is grace, is being misused. The failure now is not so much physical as psychological and spiritual: the deficiency is not the result of over-production but of mistaken production. Where the stimulus is ambition, escape, self-realization or self-advertisement, there is bound to be spiritual wastage and consequently spiritual staleness and exhaustion. Where the incentive is the love of God, there is the grace of God to carry the work along.

Thus energy diverted makes not only for impoverishment of the material produced but for impoverishment of the power which produces. The activities of a monk are ear-marked, defined, pointed. Deflected from their course they can achieve only a superficial and illusory success. It is better when they achieve no success at all, for then they are less likely to persuade their author both of his integrity and theirs. Success in a side-line activity can create in a monk a false conscience: the illusion can grow that God is setting his seal upon the work, and that the monk is doing all that is required of him in God's service.

The other aspect of work, relating particularly to the apostolate, is even more difficult to see in its true terms as defined by the setting of monasticism. In addition to the delusion of work-for-work's-sake and the more of it the better, there is here the delusion of being personally indispensable to God in the spread of his Gospel. The cause of this deviation is radically a lack of faith.[2] The danger is all the greater because the work is performed in the name of charity. The desire is not now to evade the primary obligation and to escape into works of secondary importance; the desire is now to plunge into the most important thing of all, namely charity, but to plunge nevertheless by way of escape and self-realization.

"I have seen a man running well on his course,"

[2] It must be remembered that what is said here is said primarily for monks. The religious (or the layman) whose vocation is apostolic *does* fulfil a necessary work which might not be done at all if he did not do it. God has so arranged his plan for the salvation of souls that certain graces must normally be conveyed through the medium of certain apostles. But the monk's apostolate is indirect. "Historians have vied with one another," says Montalembert (*Monks of the West,* i; p. 436), "in praising St. Benedict's genius and clear-sightedness; they have supposed that he intended to regenerate Europe, to arrest the dissolution of society, to reconstruct public order, and so on. I firmly believe that he never dreamed of regenerating anything but his own soul." The monk's apostolate, then, is primarily expressed in his work of self-sanctification.

says St. Bernard, "and then a sudden hesitation takes him . . . 'To how many,' he asks himself, 'should I be able, if I were living in my own country and neighbourhood, to communicate of that good which I enjoy here alone? . . . why is this waste made? I will go there, and in saving many I shall equally save myself. There is nothing to be feared in a mere change of place. What does it matter where I am so long as I am doing a good work? I am in fact the better placed where I am living a more useful and fruitful life.' Why repeat more of his reasoning? He goes where he wants to go, and, unhappy man, perishes. He himself comes to a miserable end and none of his own people is saved."[3] There is an almost uniform design in the progress of delusion: dissatisfaction with the stage reached in the spiritual life, longing for a quicker and more spectacular advance, discovery of a need in the world for exactly the kind of good which can be provided, justification on the grounds of fruitful labour, charity, human well-being all round.

St. Bernard further exposes this misconceived zeal for souls where he says that "a man who is making good progress in virtue, and who feels that God has poured upon him an abundance of heavenly grace, conceives a desire to preach, not indeed to his relatives and connections, but as if with a purer impulse, to strangers and to all. But yet with great prudence. He fears to

[3] *Sermons on the Canticle,* 64; 2.

incur that malediction of the prophet upon 'him who shall withhold corn from the people,' and to act against the precept of the Gospel if he should not declare from the housetops and to all what he has heard in the ear . . . it is certain and clear that to preach in public is not expedient for a monk, nor, unless he be sent, even lawful . . . therefore whatever of this nature is suggested to the mind, whether it be by your own thoughts or by the prompting of an evil spirit, recognize it always as the temptation of a subtle fox presenting evil under the appearance of good."[4]

The monk whose knowledge of God is authentic will think twice before he goes out into the world to talk about it. Indeed he will need to be sent by superiors. "To speak of the gift he has given us," writes Thomas Merton, "would seem to dissipate it and leave a stain on the pure emptiness where God's light shone . . . at the same time he [the contemplative] most earnestly wants everybody else to share his peace and joy." And again: "At no time in the spiritual life is it more necessary to become completely docile and subject to the most delicate movements of God's will and his grace than when you try to share the knowledge of his love with other men. It is far better to be so diffident that you risk not sharing it with them at all, than to throw it all away by trying to give it to other people before you have received it yourself. The contempla-

[4] *Ibid.*, 3.

97

tive who tries to preach contemplation before he himself really knows what it is, will prevent both himself
and others from finding the true path to God's peace."[5]

Another mistaken approach which lies open to the
monk is that of multiplying devotional practices to the
prejudice of the liturgy and interior prayer. The immediate cause of such a substitution may be either
scruple and superstition on the one hand, or else a
genuine desire to serve God at every possible level of
prayer on the other; but more often there is a deeper
reason for the accumulation: again there is the question
of a want of faith. The deviation taken at its most extreme will reveal a mind that trusts in its own forms
of worship, that belittles the common prayer of the
monastery, that looks to prayer for assurance rather
than for the chance of giving glory to God. If there
were more faith, there would be none of this. Whether
it goes by the name of spiritual greed, singularity, or
sheer self-will, the kind of attitude described is responsible for almost all the obstacles to monastic perfection. The reason is that the attitude springs from
pride.

When monastic perfection is taken to be a matter of
religious practices which are got through irrespective
of their Godward intention, the result is lifeless rou-

[5] *Seeds of Contemplation* (New York: New Directions, 1949),
p. 181.

tine. When it is taken to be the multiplication of duties irrespective of the sentiments which may or may not accompany them, the result again is routine. But when monastic perfection is judged in terms of quantity and sentiment the result is more serious than routine, and comes perilously close to heresy. It would be a Pelagian tenet to hold that perfection depended on man's effort, assisted, at best, by grace.

There can be a form of monastic misinterpretation which rates perfection according either to subjectivism based on emotion or to an objectivism which makes the Rule cover everything. The corrective to each extreme is a right understanding, arrived at as the result of prayer rather than study, of the relationship between effort and grace, between the value of man's work and the redeeming merits of the work of Christ.

For following the monastic ideal there must be no swerving of vision or intention. "The light of your body is your eye; if the eye is single, the whole body will be alight."[6] It is not easy to preserve the single eye, but it should not be difficult for the sincere soul to judge when the eye is beginning to veer round to another direction. Certainly the consequences give indication enough that there has been a change. We either become cynical about the virtues we are abandoning or else we become too hotly partisan about those which we are championing. In professional language

[6] Luke 11; 34.

this is called a defense-mechanism; in effect it means that we tend to decry those things in which we have failed, and canonize those in whose service we suspect our true motive.

To be a success as a writer or preacher is no compensation for being a failure as a monk. A monk exists for the glory of God, and everything that he does is to be valued in the light of this. All other works and purposes are deviations. A monk is not called to convert the world by the power which he exerts over souls; he is called to do battle in his own soul, and the degree to which he yields the victory to grace will be the degree to which he influences the conversion of others. A monk does not work at the service of God in order to attract followers, still less in order to attract fans, but in order to love God more and to express God's love in the world about him. People who try hard enough can usually be successful, and people who keep their wits about them can usually become popular, but in order to fulfil the monastic vocation a soul needs something more than constant application and social consciousness. To be a true monk a man will need to follow God's grace at every point. "The state of union," and it is towards this that monasticism directs the soul, "lies in a total transformation of the will into the will of God, so that there is nothing in the soul that is contrary to the will of God, but that, in all and through all, its activity is that of the will of God alone."[7] This brings us to interior simplicity, which is the subject-matter of the second half of this work.

[7] St. John of the Cross, *Ascent of Mount Carmel,* Bk. I; ch. 11, 1

BOOK TWO

Approach from the Inside

6

Simplicity of Vision

WHEN WE HAVE gone through the catalogue of outward
realities, we are left with the much shorter catalogue of
the soul's inward responses to monasticism's inward
appeal. Thus it might be said that advance in the monastic vocation is nothing else than the deepening of the
idea of charity. By obedience, by prayer, by experience
of suffering and of community life, the soul comes to
amplify and extend the implication until charity covers
the whole horizon which it is seen to have created and
ordered. The soul sees charity not only as something
coming from God and due to God, but as God himself:
Deus caritas est. The impulse on which my vocation is
launched does not belong to me: *charitas Christi urget
nos*.

Such an understanding of charity as the unifying
force of the religious life, the breath which gives it
existence, has practical significance. The soul, learning
in the early stages that sanctity does not consist in the
accumulation of more and more devout practices but
in the purer and purer practice of what is laid down,

comes to know—later on, when dryness has robbed monastic service of enthusiasm and even perhaps of meaning—that the solution is not to get back to the attitude of mind which was enjoyed in the novitiate. The solution, both for the beginner and for the more advanced, is always the solution of charity. The novice learns to do from the motive of love all that he would otherwise be doing out of routine or self-interest; the professed monk aims at doing out of love all that as a novice he had done out of sentiment, natural energy, novelty or automatic response.

Whenever we are granted a light on the religious vocation we almost always want to go back to the point of departure, to the stage at which in retrospect we see ourselves to have followed a false scent. We imagine we can make a new start as though nothing had happened since. But these returns in spirit are apt to be artificial; there is too much of the memory and imagination about them, not enough of the intellect and will. We cannot put the milk back in the cocoanut. Experience has come between us and our original discovery. There is no novitiate revisited; the emotion is not there any more and it may not be re-created. To make the attempt at building up an atmosphere which helped at the time is to lose the opportunity of meeting the existing reality. Present realities are far more helpful to spiritual progress than remembered atmospheres. A man who has all he can do to hold one rope in his hand would be a fool to try grasping another which he once held but which has now swung away from him. Give us *this* day our daily bread, not the bread we ate as novices. The actual is the bread of God, the will of God.

Yet it is the actual which we dread, and the remembered which brings us comfort and hope. Reality, seen against an idealized past, strikes fear. Reality may immediately cause boredom or disgust, but fear—fear of things getting worse—is the effect which present realities have more significantly the power to produce. It is a mistake to look to the past even for standards of comparison, let alone for directions which will help us to pursue our ever-developing desire. The whole point about the life of faith is that our standards of comparison tell us nothing, and that our directions point nowhere. The life of faith is meant to draw us, past bewilderment and discouragement and self-pity, so that eventually we lose our loneliness in the presence of God's love.

Love is the fulfilment of monasticism as well as of the law. It is the justification of monasticism, and its criterion. Twice in the fourth chapter of his Rule love is spoken of by St. Benedict as being the primary purpose of the life. *Nihil amori Christi praeponere*,[1] and again *in primis Dominum Deum diligere ex toto corde, tota anima, tota virtute*.[2] St. Benedict comes back to

[1] "To prefer nothing to Christ."
[2] "In the first place to love the Lord God with all one's heart, all one's soul, and all one's strength."

the same idea, which gives the essence of his doctrine, where he says in the seventy-second chapter, *Christo omnino nihil praeponant.* Once this substantial quality is grasped, the regulations assume their right relation to the life as a whole. If love is the theme, the expression of love will lie in faithful obedience to rule. In what else? "If you love me, keep my commandments."

When a St. Benedict of Aniane, a St. Robert of Molesme, a St. Bernard of Clairvaux raises his voice to challenge the existing laxity of his age, it is not simply that he is a perfectionist and cannot abide the discrepancy between the ideal as proposed in the letter and the interpretation as borne out in its practice; it is much more because he sees monasticism as a matter of love. His experience has taught him that the best way to attain to love, to prove love, to invite and impart love is to be faithful to the principles laid down in black and white by the man raised up by God to found the order.

Love and law go together. While there may be law without love, there certainly cannot be love without law. For the perfecting of law there must be love. If we examine the spirit of those who, more recently than the saints cited above, have recalled monasticism to its primitive purpose, we see the authentic inspiration of praise and charity. Though the Church has not set the official seal of sanctity upon them, the work of such men as Dom Nicolas Fanson of Saint-Hubert (c. 1635),

Dom Benedict van Haeften of Afflighem (d. 1648), Armand de Rancé of La Trappe (d. 1700), Dom Guéranger of Solesmes (d. 1875), Dom Maurus Wolter of Beuron (d. 1890) has St. Benedict's *ut in omnibus glorificetur Deus* as its sole foundation. In our own time we see the same spirit at work in the heroic return to the Rule made by Dom Alexis Presse in his foundation of Cistercians of the Common Observance at Boquen in Brittany, and by Dom Gregorio Lemercier in his Benedictine foundation at Cuernavaca in Mexico. None of these communities could have been founded, much less maintained, on a regard for the Rule without love. The text of the Rule may satisfy the antiquarian and even launch an experiment, but if the Rule is to live, and if souls are to be influenced by it, *nihil amori Christi praeponere* must be taken as its principle first and last. Charity: Christ's love—expressed towards the Father in praise, and towards man in the community life. The monastic purpose is not a complex one; all it asks is a single-minded fidelity in its pursuit. Lending itself all too readily to multiplicity and concentration upon the minutiae, the religious life nevertheless takes its stand upon the direct approach to God. In the complexity of contemporary affairs the need to recognize this fact is all the greater. Throughout the history of monasticism the reformers who were successful were those who, refusing to look to right or left, put their heads down and went straight for the one thing necessary. They were obstinate because they knew that they were right. All reformers know that they are right, but only those who have the love of God as their primary object are blessed by God in their reforms.

But there can be self-deception in all this: we can pretend that love is our aim and guiding principle when in fact it is not. On the assumption that our wills are in the right direction we can allow ourselves to be controlled by our emotions. St. Augustine's "love and do what you will" becomes an excuse for licence, and our Lord's words are made to read "if you love me, forget my commandments."

As soon as we begin to move away from the pure course of charity we find ourselves doing all those things which monastic simplicity and liberty are supposed to avoid. We compensate for our want of love by performing acts which denote but which do not express love. At one extreme we can separate ourselves from our brethren on the plea that we must devote our whole attention to God; at the other extreme we exaggerate our social responsibilities to the detriment of the interior life. Shutting one eye does not simplify the vision; it only prejudices the perspective. The law of charity is as clear as the heavens; the ideal of the Rule is as uncompromising as a mountain. But we can neglect to look up at the heavens; we can try to get round the mountain. The result is that the sky clouds over and we cannot see it when we want to; the mountain shrinks to a mole-hill.

Charity is one thing, and the Rule is one thing. The moment we become selective in our charity, the virtue falls apart. The moment we become selective in our Rule, the ideal falls apart. If there is simplicity and unity in charity which is the end, there is also simplicity and unity in the Rule which, for the monk, is the means. People praise the Rule of St. Benedict as allowing many different observances, as being adaptable to many different ideals. But experience shows that whenever the unity of the Rule is tampered with, the specifically Benedictine ideal is lost. The holy Rule hangs together in such a way that to take out any one essential point of its doctrine is to collapse the whole. "Let all therefore follow the Rule in all things," says the author himself, "and let no man rashly depart from it."[3] The only hope for the Rule, then, is to keep it.

Simplicity of vision reveals itself also in steadfastness and a certain realism which refuses to fill a felt void with romantic conceptions of monasticism. As we grow older in the religious life we tend to become increasingly conscious of our insufficiency. Admitting ourselves to be failures, and imagining that to do so must denote the possession of humility in its perfection, we begin to compare ourselves with other monks. This

[3] Ch. 3. See also 60, 62, 73.

leads either to envy and discouragement on the one hand, or to pride and false security on the other. "As the moth gnaws away a garment," says St. John Chrysostom, "so does envy consume a man." Envy, driving a man back upon himself in bitterness, makes true humility impossible. A man may envy not only another man but another vocation, another life. The envious man can grow to be so restless from envying the observance of other monasteries that his own observance in his own monastery becomes a torture to him. He tries to compensate by imitating the observance which he sees in other monasteries, and his life becomes a stage act—perfect perhaps in its performance but lacking in reality, simplicity, truth. "The envious man shall not be a partaker of wisdom."[4] "The eye of the envious is full of malice; he turns away his face, and despises his own soul."[5] It is the wrong sort of despising because he is looking for the wrong sort of satisfaction.

Just as fulfilling the Gospel is something more than following an imaginary Christ, so fulfilling the Rule is something more than following an imaginary vocation. If we follow the real Christ and do his actual will, we should be ready also to accept the Rule as an existing reality and obey its implications in the actual setting of our lives. The religious life is the life of faith, and this is for some where faith hurts most. It is only faith

[4] Wisd. 6; 25.
[5] Ecclus. 14; 8.

that can resolve the problem of the soul's failure and frustrated aspiration. A monk has to live with himself, has to go on in the twofold knowledge of what he might be and what he is. For him there is no escape into distraction; the battle goes on in his own soul. The monk has to cross and re-cross the broken battle-fields of his monastic life, the ugly terrain of disillusion, wanderlust, blocked hope and wasted opportunity. The tragedy is that he can let himself be trapped there, in his own bad-lands, instead of living above it all in faith.

Faith is the only way to this harmony of spirit which we have called simplicity and unity. Where there is faith there is no need to act a part—even to oneself. Since faith looks to God and not to self, the necessity for building up one's own private securities does not come up. Self is nothing, so there is nothing to compensate for. Sincerity, as surely as humility, is a facet of truth and follows truth. *Sine cera*—without the wax which went to fill in the flaws of the marble when the Romans started to carve in the manner of the Greeks. Sincerity means that there is nothing to disguise: the material, as he has made it, stands open before God.

Our mistake as monks is to take our supernatural vocation, our life of faith, for granted. We know that our lives are orientated towards God, and we leave the thing at that. But it must be more than a notional assumption; it must be a living inspiration. Faith is a fact of grace but it is also an act, a movement, a dynamic. Often we tell ourselves that the reason why we produce no results is because we are living the life of faith and should not expect to produce results. In reality it may well be that we are half asleep. The Cistercian commentator, Isaac of Stella, draws the distinction between the *otium* of the true contemplative soul and the *otiositas* of the false. In his fourteenth sermon he says that among the many monks who are freed from the solicitudes of Martha so that they may give themselves to the devotion of Mary, there are yet many who are prostrate with the torpor of Lazarus. The conclusion to be drawn from this authority is that the more withdrawn and regular the monastic life, the greater the danger of deluding oneself about the life of faith.[6]

When so many hazards abound, how shall we find security? The answer, as St. Benedict says it does, must lie in Christ. By setting ourselves to follow unequivocally his word we guard against listening to the voices which explain away his word. His word will tell us where to look, and then we must walk while we have the light. He who is the way and the truth and the life will command the simplicity of our vision.

[6] "Where are they who doze over their books in the cloister, who sleep when the lessons are being read in choir and at the living voice of the sermon in chapter?" Quoted from his fellow Cistercian by Thomas Merton in some conference notes issued privately.

7

The Work of Solitude

EXTERIOR AND INTERIOR solitude have each to be considered as elements of the monastic life. Each plays a part in the activity of contemplation: exterior solitude ensures the setting or condition, interior solitude provides the disposition. Exterior solitude is the physical state sought by the soul as a means most conducive to prayer. Interior solitude is an attitude of mind, brought about by grace, which combines tranquillity, detachment, and longing for union with God alone.

The need and desire for exterior solitude can be seen as the consequence of conversion from worldliness to the service of God. The soul longs to be separated from creatures so that God may become the sole object of desire. "If it be embarrassed by anything and set upon anything," says St. John of the Cross, "the will is not free, solitary, and pure in the way necessary for divine transformation."[1] The soul sees at the outset of the spiritual life that a measure of solitude is absolutely necessary, is indeed the element in which interior graces

[1] *Ascent of Mount Carmel,* Bk. I; ch. 11.

are responded to and the will of God more clearly appreciated.

Solitude will accordingly be pursued and cherished, not as an end but as an environment. It is chosen as the environment furthest removed from the world. Then, as the interior life develops and the soul becomes accustomed to the separations and to being alone, solitude is thought of not so much as something from which the world is excluded but rather as an element in its own right. The world is not the norm; solitude is the norm. The universe was solitary before the world invaded its isolation. The first human beings, alone together in the Garden of Eden before the fall, were solitary before sin made privacy something to be secured. The first monks were solitary, fleeing the world but possessing positively the freedom of the desert. We would do better to think of the world as lacking the due environment of solitude than to think of solitude as escaping the business of the world.

When the monk has learned the secrets of solitude, when he has come to terms with his loneliness, he will find himself able, when obliged to mix with the world, to take with him his own solitude and live within it in recollection. He will have learned, without having consciously acquired a technique, how to keep sheltered his essential self in the midst of distraction. But even so, it would be foolish for him to take risks; solitude can be easily dissipated. The monk, like Ruskin's artist, should be "fit for the best society of men, and keep out of it."

If example were needed to show the work of disposing the soul for contemplation, there is the example of St. Benedict himself. Not only did he begin his monastic life as a hermit, but in legislating for monks he allowed for the eremitical vocation as a development which in certain cases might arise out of the cenobitic.

But it is not only for the sake of peace that a man withdraws himself from noise and creatures. He wants to be forgotten as much as he wants to forget. If a man seeks solitude only for the glamour which he sees in it, he is not seeking to be hidden but to be known. He is not seeking to be lost in God but to be discovered in the minds of men. It is a form of ostentation. There is always a certain lure about solitude, and a soul must learn by the light of grace to distinguish between the true and false yearning for it. False solitude draws a man in upon himself and gets between his soul and God. False solitude is a preoccupation, a bitterness; true solitude is a liberation.

The fruits of true solitude are manifest at once: indifference to the appeal of worldly entertainments and pleasures; increasing purity of intention with regard to outward as well as inward works; unselfconsciousness in the exercise of virtue; greater objectivity in prayer; instinctive confidence in God and corresponding independence of self. "In solitude she lived," sings St.

John of the Cross in the *Spiritual Canticle,* "and in solitude built her nest." These first two lines of the thirty-fifth stanza give us the work of the soul in establishing exterior solitude. The lines which complete the stanza give us the work of grace establishing the soul in interior solitude: "And in solitude, alone, hath the Beloved guided her. In solitude also wounded her with love."

But the nest has to be built; it is not handed to the soul ready made. Silence has to be cultivated, and a serious effort made to withdraw from anything that is likely to jar upon the spirit. Interior silence is impossible without exterior silence, and in this matter of silence and solitude it is the whole man who is involved —spirit and sense. St. Bernard speaks of silence as "the guardian of the monastic life,"[2] so it is the whole vocation that is involved—corporate and individual.

Just as monastic poverty guards the monastery and the monk against the worries which are occasioned by wealth, monastic silence guards monastery and monk against the disturbances which are occasioned by talk and outward affairs. Silence, solitude, enclosure: guardians of the monastic purpose. It is difficult to see how monasticism could exist without these safeguards; they are almost as necessary to it as the vows themselves. Indeed they are so closely connected with the vows as to

[2] *Sermons for the Seasons;* sermon 2 for the octave of the Epiphany.

deserve examination in the light of Benedictine obedience, stability, and conversion of manners. How does my silence, or the lack of it, reflect upon the submission which I owe to superiors and the principles laid down in the holy Rule? Is stability represented in my observance of enclosure? Does conversion of manners show itself in the separations which I make from the world and the care which I give to ensuring solitude?

It is important for monks, Benedictine and Cistercian monks especially, to realize that this solitude is not a subtraction from the common life but rather something added to it. The point is brought out clearly by Father Thomas Merton where he says: "It is because the monks enable one another to live most easily and peacefully in solitude and silence, because they provide for one another an atmosphere of recollection and solitude and prayer, that they are able to achieve the supreme end of the monastic life."[3] The strength of solitude is a combined strength, arising out of the individual spirituality of each monk every bit as much as it arises out of the seclusion of the place. The same author, and in a more poetic passage, says further: ". . . the silence of the forest, the peace of the early morning wind moving in the branches of the trees, the solitude and isolation of the house of God: these are good because it is in silence, and not in commotion, in solitude and not in

[3] *The Silent Life* (New York: Farrar, Straus and Cudahy, 1957), p. 36.

crowds, that God best likes to reveal himself to men . . .
each one contributes his share in peace and recollection."[4]

In St. Bernard's sermons, particularly where the saint
is talking about the tabernacles and courts of God's
house, there is the same idea of a holy solitude built
up by the holiness of the brethren living together in
solitude. St. Bernard takes the soul from court to court,
from exterior to interior solitude, until the final consummation is arrived at in the soul's union with God.
"Here on earth we have the tabernacles which are the
lowest of these spiritual dwellings . . . the courts constitute an intermediate place, the place of expectation,
whilst you are yourself the home of thanksgiving and
praise . . . in the first are found the first-fruits of the
spirit, in the second the riches of the spirit, in the third
the fulness of the spirit . . . men are made saints in the
first, find security in the second, and attain to complete
happiness in the third."[5]

Though St. Bernard made a great point of enclosure
—among the first of his requirements, for example,
upon the affiliation of monasteries of black monks to
Cîteaux, was the abandonment of apostolic work and
extra-claustral activity of any kind—he has more to
say of inward than of outward solitude. For him the

[4] *Ibid.,* p. 37.
[5] *Sermons for the Seasons;* sermon 4 for the dedication of a
church.

main concern is to draw the soul away from the desire of creatures and into inward unity. The physical seclusion involved is a subject rather for the "consuetudinary" than for the chapter conference. When the soul can say with the bride in St. John of the Cross's *Canticle* "in the inner cellar of my beloved have I drunk,"[6] the measures needed to keep solitary the approaches to that cellar are taken for granted. Instinctively the crowds are left behind, for now "the bride has entered the pleasant and desirable garden"[7] and the secrets of interior solitude are learned.

It is important to understand that interior solitude is not a dead thing, empty because cut off from outside supply. Far from being sterile it is productive: it produces tranquillity where external solitude merely conditions it. *Vacate*—and if it stopped at that it would indeed be a negative quality, but it goes on—*et videte quoniam ego sum Deus.*[8] Interior solitude assumes a presence and proposes an activity. Where God is present it would be a mistake to think of interior solitude as emptiness. Where recollection is going on it would be a mistake to think of inaction. We speak loosely of solitude as a certain holy loneliness in God, and as far as it goes the term gives the general sense of it, but if this

[6] Stanza 26.

[7] Stanza 22.

[8] Psalm 45; 9.

suggests homesickness or a hankering for company it is misleading. A better idea is given, though it sounds clumsy, by speaking of aloneness with God. The soul stands solitary, and is content to stand solitary, but God is there.

This inward contentment with isolation is not something which the monk can bring about simply by achieving exterior solitude. It is as much as the monk can do to answer the summons *vacate,* and the greater part of this is effected in the night of the senses, while to comply adequately with the second clause, *videte,* he will depend entirely upon the light of grace. The *videte* is the introduction to the illuminative way.

As exterior solitude corresponds with the purgative, so interior solitude corresponds with the illuminative way. It is conceivably possible, though unlikely, that the way of purgation and the night of the senses could effect the necessary changes in the soul without the help of physical, actual, solitude; it is not conceivable that the illuminative and unitive ways could be followed by one who lacked interior solitude.

Just as the light granted in the illuminative way eclipses the light of worldly wisdom, so the peace and order brought about by interior solitude subdues the disorder of worldly desires. Interior solitude not only sees but silences. It sees deeper into the will of God, into the meaning of his inspired word, into the significance of the created order, into the mystery of suffering.

And at the same time it subdues the emotions and passions. Nor is it that the soul sees first, and then decides to subdue. Rather the very act of appreciating the implications of grace is itself responsible for the subjection of what is contrary to grace. This act is itself the action of grace. I see now not I, but Christ sees through the eyes of my soul; I subdue now not I, but Christ subdues for me.

Having come to the state of interior solitude by the way of exterior solitude, the soul controls outward desires by the development of the one desire which is within. This is illustrated in St. Bernard by the simile of the spider, which, when the web is damaged, does its mending from within itself, from the centre of its spinning, and not at the actual break. We enter into our solitude by means of positive separations, and once at home and at peace we further establish our interior enclosure by the continued act of responding to grace. "I longed that a vital fluid should be poured into all my veins and into the very marrow of my bones," confesses St. Bernard of his search after God, "so that it should be detached from all other affections and know only this." When he had found the union which he sought, he had found also the interior solitude which detached him from all other affections.

This is not to claim that interior solitude is immune from every invasion. The powers of evil do not let the matter go at that. Temptation will attack the soul as

much as ever it did, and probably more. But within the
essential cell there will be greater reserves to draw from;
the tranquillity which was the outcome of silence and
recollection will come to the rescue. The higher faculties will find themselves composed enough to see the
light of grace through the storm, and will be strong
enough to command the lower. There is all the difference between disturbance and disorder. There is no
part of the soul that may not be subjected to disturbance, but where there is interior solitude in the sense
discussed there cannot but be order. Mary was disturbed on at least two occasions in her life, but never for
a moment was her soul disordered. It was not the hidden life alone, lived in the obscurity of Nazareth, which
guaranteed her calm in the face of puzzlement and
anxiety; it was her solitude of heart, her "aloneness"
with God. Only those who possess God can be truly
self-possessed.

The conclusions to be drawn, then, are as follows.
First that solitude is not a mere adjunct to the monastic
life but a necessary part of it. It is something which the
individual monk may have to secure for himself: not all
monasteries are so secluded that they can provide it for
him. He should know that natural attraction or aversion
to solitude has nothing to do with it: what matters is his
recognition of its necessity and his will to see it through.
He should know too that *by itself* retreat from the world

and from creatures is without value: the void must be filled with the presence of God. Abstraction for the sake of abstraction has nothing supernatural about it, may even be rather unnatural. The rule is simple: empty solitude produces lifeless work, prayerful solitude produces prayerful and worthwhile work. Finally, all exterior solitude is related to interior solitude, and interior solitude is immediately related to grace.

The above is borne out by the teaching of Francisco de Osuna in his classic work *The Third Spiritual Alphabet*. In his fifteenth treatise, the author enumerates three things necessary for contemplation. The first of these may be described here in his own words (though somewhat condensed); the other two will appear in subsequent chapters.

"The first requisite is the place, which must be fitting, retired, and quiet, for we know that the Jews were blamed for being in the streets, and the angel bade Lot remove from the neighbourhood of Sodom and seek safety on the mountain. Abraham was told to go out from his kindred and ordered to go into the land of vision, and God bade the patriarch Jacob arise and go to Bethel, which means the house of God. God also commanded the chosen people to leave Egypt and dwell with him, implying that he could dwell better with them in the land of promise. He also bade the prophet Moses ascend the mountain to die, showing that the farther we withdraw from the world the better can we die to it and live with God. St. Antony and St. Antoninus left their homes as being places unsuited to prayer. Our Lord went into the mountains and desert places in order to pray more quietly. He did this not on his own account but to teach us by his example to seek for solitary spots, favourable for compunction and silence, withdrawn from the tumults and excitement of the world."[9] Certainly God is present in the market-place and in the plain, but souls are drawn to meet him more intimately in his own dwelling and on the mountain.

De Osuna gives us the key to this doctrine where he cites the vocation of Abraham: the summons is to the land of *vision*. To leave one's kindred is only half the battle for solitude; the main work is that of seeing when one has got there. Yet it is only in interior solitude that one *does* see. De Osuna does not mention it, but the incident—so casually given in the wider context of the story as hardly to attract the notice of commentators—of Isaac meditating in the evening, after his camels have been watered and when his camp is at rest, suggests exactly the same idea. Isaac is in the desert, he has withdrawn himself from the bustle of the tents, and he comes upon the well "which is called of the living and the seeing."[10] The desert by itself will not help him—it is

[9] Translated from the Spanish by the Benedictines of Stanbrook (New York: Benziger, 1931), pp. 303-304.
[10] Gen. 24; 62-63.

in fact a place of menace—but the well can help him.
Interior solitude is precisely such a well in the exterior
solitude of the desert. Its shaft is walled, and it contains
living water—water which gives vision as well as life.

8

The Specifically
Monastic Virtues

THOSE MONASTIC VIRTUES which relate directly or indirectly to the vows will be dealt with in the next
chapter. In the present chapter will be considered the
more marked among the qualities which the combined
effect of prayer and the common life should develop in
the soul. Since the list of such virtues might be extended
indefinitely, and since any selection is bound to be
arbitrary, no claim is made here to a full-scale treatment
of the subject. The aim is simply to lay stress upon certain characteristics which set the seal of authenticity
upon the vocation—or, to put it the other way round,
would go seriously against the monastic life if they were
lacking.

If Christian perfection finds a particular expression
in monastic perfection, Christian charity will find its
particular expression in monastic charity. We are talking now of charity to one's neighbour. In a monastery
there is the twofold duty of charity arising out of a twofold relationship with others: the charity demanded by

the community life, and the charity demanded by hospitality and the spiritual needs of souls. Whatever the monk's response to solitude, there will always be his brethren to whom he extends Christ's love. Whatever the monastery's tradition of seclusion, there will always be guests and people who look to the monks for direction.

If the common life in the monastery is not the exchange of Christ's love, then not only is every other activity which is exercised there—its liturgy, its contemplation, its manual or other labour, its penance—empty of meaning, but the common life itself is nothing more than aggregation. If the life is to be towards God at all, the bond must be charity.[1] A house may have a great name for learning, may even perform the outward acts of hospitality, may spend itself in what passes in the eyes of the world for martyrdom, but if it have not charity it is nothing.[2]

St. Bernard distinguishes between the charity of infusion and the charity of effusion. Effusive charity can be exercised safely and with a pure intention only when it is drawing from its infused reserves.[3] "Let all your works," says St. Paul, "be done in charity."[4] There is a difference between charitable works and works done in

[1] Cf. Col. 3; 14.
[2] Cf. I Cor. 13; 1-5.
[3] *Sermons on the Canticle*, 18.
[4] I Cor. 16; 14.

charity. Works done in charity further the virtue which prompts them; they further moreover the love of God as well as the love of others. This is where de Osuna's second requirement for contemplation comes in. "The second thing that helps the spiritual life," says de Osuna, "is good company . . . it is a characteristic of virtuous men that they should live with others like themselves. Holy companions help greatly to free us from the trials felt by the lonely in the spiritual life, for it is easier to pray for an hour with the devout than with the self-indulgent and talkative . . . you will suffer by associating with the dissipated, but will forfeit nothing with the recollected."[5] Where the monk's charity is true, his recollection follows. Charity cannot but be the first effect, as it is intended to be the first foundation, of monasticism. Almost on the last page of his Rule, and therefore as his considered legacy, St. Benedict exhorts his monks as follows: "Let them cherish fraternal charity with love, fear God, love their abbot with sincere and humble affection, and prefer nothing whatever to Christ."[6]

Whatever interferes with fraternal charity is therefore the enemy of the monastic spirit. Exclusiveness, thoughtlessness, snobbishness, bitterness: all these are attacks upon monasticism. A common offence in community life is wanting to get ahead of another, and,

[5] *Op. cit.,* pp. 304-305.
[6] Ch. 72.

when this desire is not realized, wanting the other to do badly in the work which was angled for. More failures in charity, and therefore in monastic spirit, are due to envy than is generally supposed. We become so easily dispirited at the sight of our own failure that we first envy the success of others, and then, as a compensation, begin to belittle it. "Since we cannot attain to greatness," wrote the cynical Montaigne, "let us revenge ourselves by railing at it." Sadly rather than cynically the same idea is expressed by Aeschylus: "Few have the strength of character to rejoice, without a touch of envy, in a friend's success."

In virtue of our monastic life, then, we should be easier to live with in the monastery than we were in the world. More tolerant, more considerate, even perhaps more courteous. The Christ-life should show itself in good manners as well as in the more heroic and self-sacrificing virtues. Our prayer develops our charity, and our charity develops our prayer; in the joint movement of love we mount to love itself. By charity of the spirit we serve one another,[7] and serving one another we fulfil the law of Christ.

The connection between charity and humility is so close that to describe a monk as a good community man is to say that he does not thrust himself forward—that he makes his contribution, but not in such a way that all must acknowledge the superiority of his contribution.

[7] Cf. Gal. 5; 13.

The monk who is charitable and humble does not compare his contribution, or his character, or his ideals, or his perfection with what he sees in others. He knows that the value of a man and his work is according to the amount of light received from God, and the amount of love with which that light is followed. He knows that, short of a divine revelation, this information about another's life will be withheld from him. So he does not judge. This is humility and charity working as one.

Just as the monk cannot lose by charity, so neither can he lose by being humble. In union with Christ who humbled himself, becoming obedient unto death, the monk is not only safest when acting in humility but safe *only* when acting in humility. The moment he acts arrogantly, in self-will, he steps outside the humility of Christ and is left to work out the consequences of his self-interest and self-opinion. "When you pass through a low doorway," says St. Bernard, "you have nothing to fear from stooping, however low you stoop; but if you raise your head higher than the doorway, though but by the width of a finger, you strike against the frame and injure yourself. So also with the soul: there is nothing to be feared from humbling yourself to however great an extent, but much more to be feared from even the least presumptuous self-exaltation."[8]

The monk should not have to force himself to acts of humility to prove his virtue; his virtue should make

[8] *Sermons on the Canticle,* 13.

133

him choose to be hidden, ready to be humbled, happy to be neglected and forgotten in the manoeuvre for position. Obscurity has, to the monk, the right sort of feel; he is at home in it. The word "humility" comes from *humus,* and the closer to the earth the better for the monk: he is levelled, self-effaced. If a study of St. Benedict's chapter on the degrees of humility does not convince a monk of the necessity of self-effacement, nothing will.

With humility goes inevitably the indifference to praise or blame which is one of the most marked characteristics of sanctity. "To appear admirable to others, and to think humbly of oneself," says St. Bernard, "this I judge to be the most marvellous among the virtues."[9] So marvellous is it, and so rarely seen apart from examples of singular holiness, that it comes as a telling proof of its supernatural quality: humility is a grace to be prayed for. Humility is not learned out of a book; it has to be burned in by experience, and spared from the corroding process of discouragement by love.

When love has shaped the soul's humility, criticism and malicious opposition have no longer any power to hurt. The soul, though far from being insensitive, is living above the disturbance. The soul is glad to be identified with the surrender of Christ to the hostility of the Jews.

Another quality which should characterize the mo-

[9] *Ibid.*

nastic life is a certain imperturbability of mind which rides the tempests both of sorrow and temptation. Agitation, in the sense of fuss, is not of God. One cannot imagine Christ in the state of such an agitation. Serenity is not only the disposition for spiritual gifts but invariably the consequence. "When these joys come from God," says St. Teresa, "they come laden with love and strength that aid the soul on its way, and increase its good works and virtues."[10] Serenity must be cultivated, guarded, and as far as possible imparted.

"Whatsoever shall befall the just man, it shall not make him sad."[11] And again: "Give not up thy soul to sadness, and afflict not thyself in thine own counsel. The joyfulness of the heart is the life of a man. Drive away sadness far from thee, for it hath killed many and there is no profit in it."[12] It is not that sadness disappears as men grow holier, but that with increasing holiness goes an increasing appreciation of the meaning and necessity of suffering. The joys of the saints are both more spiritual and more according to right reason, and are therefore found to be more compensating for the inescapable sadnesses of life.

The sorrows of the more advanced soul, moreover, are felt at a different level and are occasioned by different provocation from those suffered in the earlier stages

12 Ecclus. 30; 22-25.
11 Prov. 12; 21.
12 Ecclus. 30; 22-25.

of the spiritual life. St. Teresa, who was certainly not by nature melancholy, admits that we shall go on feeling our sorrows "until we come to the land where nothing can grieve us any more."[13] But in the same paragraph she explains that the cause of our grief, "increasing in proportion to the divine grace received," will be sorrow for sin and the thought of our ingratitude and failure to respond to God's love. This is exactly in line with St. Benedict's doctrine of compunction which he repeats again and again throughout the holy Rule. The problem for most monks is to balance their joys and sorrows in such a way that joy does not become an end in itself and a dissipation, and that sorrow does not become dispiriting. Melancholy is always an evil to be guarded against in monasteries, but if the principles of serenity, confidence in God, participation in Christ's sufferings are understood, the effect of natural sadness will not be something morbid but something sanctifying. It is only when sorrow is self-regarding that it shows itself to be a menace to spirituality and the monastic life. The sorrow that is self-forgetting, that leads to compassion for other people's sorrows, is a stimulus to spirituality and the monastic life.

The last of the virtues to be discussed here as being particularly necessary to the monastic life, and as being the product of the monastic life rightly lived, is at once the most obvious and the most subtle of the list pre-

[13] *Op. cit.*, 6th mansion; ch. 7.

sented. Faith. *Of course* you would expect faith to be needed in the pursuit of monastic perfection; *of course* you would expect monastic perfection to deepen the life of faith. Yes, but here we are considering in the monk a particular aspect of faith which has to meet a particular aspect of unfaith.

The difficulty in the case of most monks, and certainly in the case of all monks not engaged in directly apostolic work, is to go on serving God when there is nothing to show that the service is doing any good. This is where faith is needed, where the supernatural purpose must supply for the lack of natural returns. This kind of faith is all the more necessary in an age which has canonized output and which is consequently nervous about waste. If the danger to monasteries in the Middle Ages was the misuse of leisure, the danger today is the misuse of work. Activism is as serious a threat to monasticism as idleness.

Once granted that the monk does not exist for the purpose of producing visible results, it calls for great faith in the monk to see religious of other orders (or of his own) producing results and at the same time to renounce the satisfaction of achievement in his own case. He is tempted to feel that his powers are wasted, that the work of the choir and of contemplation is of doubtful value when compared with the work of winning souls to Christ. What he has to accept, and accept in faith, is that the work of the choir and contemplation *is* work for souls.

How, without this kind of faith in his vocation *as a life of faith,* will the monk be content with pulling up turnips when he might be preaching? How will the scholar or spiritual writer avoid the sense of waste when he sweeps his cell instead of getting a servant to do it for him, and so leave him more time for study? How will the efficient administrator sit through long offices in choir when there are no figures in the books to give the findings? What makes the monk who is a farmer, a technician, a schoolmaster, a professor, a scientist—any specialist you care to mention—what makes him suspend his natural activity? Why does a spiritual director feel confident that in answering the letter of a six-year-old child he is serving God as effectively as when he writes to those who consult him in their spiritual difficulties? The resolving factor in all these things is faith. Once a monk loses this sense of supernatural purpose in the work in hand, he begins immediately to talk about waste, and what are our talents given us for, and the great thing is to do something worth while.

A development of this very necessary monastic faith is to be seen in the readiness with which the monk sacrifices his leisure, the time which he feels drawn to use for prayer, at the demand of obedience or charity. It calls for a high degree of faith to substitute exterior duty for interior attraction. But the interior solitude which the combined activity of grace and personal effort has built up in the soul is here the monk's refuge, and he performs his outward obligations from inward re-serves. Indeed it is in interior solitude that such a faith as we are discussing is enlarged and matured.

In the same spirit of confidence in God's wisdom the soul accepts any other deprivations, unreasonable though they appear on the surface, which necessity ex-acts. The removal of a spiritual director on whose guidance one had absolutely relied, the loss of sympathy and understanding on the part of those who had seen one's point of view, the changes of policy and common purpose in the house—these and many others like them are occasions for the exercise of faith. Perhaps as a man grows older in religion the need for faith in God alone as the solution of his problem—monastic problem as well as personal—increases. He finds himself getting out of touch with the ever-developing thought of the com-munity. Perhaps even out of sympathy. Here is at last the supreme test: is he going to surrender himself to self-pity, cynicism, isolation of heart, or is he going to surrender himself to God? He has now, at this trial of his faith, the chance of proving the quality of his charity, his solitude, his hope. One way or the other his spiritual course, developed over the years and become to him second nature, will be shown up. It means either hardening in selfishness or mellowing in charity. If self-commiseration is the mark of defeat in the test, grati-tude to God for the grace of the religious vocation and for all that the vocation has involved is the mark of triumph. It is the mark of humility and love, which are the substance of monasticism.

9

The Inwardness
of the Vows

As GIVEN BY St. Benedict in his fifty-eighth chapter the monastic vows are those of stability, conversion of life, and obedience. Though not mentioned specifically, poverty and chastity are included in the vows of obedience and conversion. In the examination which follows, the five separate obligations will be treated in the order as they appear above, but once again the reader is reminded that the approach, in line with the rest of the book, is interior and personal rather than theological, historical, or legal.

Without the ideal of stability the whole structure of Benedictinism falls apart. There are almost as many factors in the monastery as in the world that militate against the perfect observance of stability; if there were not a vow to safeguard it, monastic stability would disintegrate under pressure. It is chiefly the pressures which come from within that Benedictine stability is designed to meet; the pressures which come from without are for the most part determined by either obedience or necessity. If psychological instability can be controlled, the ideal has triumphed. The monk whose will is bent upon continuing in the monastery of his profession until he dies has little to fear on the score of St. Benedict's first vow. St. Benedict himself made several changes in the course of his monastic career, but he was certainly not lacking in stability. St. Benedict deliberately left one form of monastic life in order to undertake another, he chose to abandon an unworthy community because he knew that his influence was having no effect, he left one of his own foundations rather than submit to a particular form of persecution. Yet stability was for him the essence of his Rule. Of St. Bernard it may also be said that while circumstances forced him away from his original anchorage, and sometimes kept him separated for considerable periods from any sort of local anchorage, his stability not only remained intact but developed, under these very pressures, to full perfection.

So, on the showing of the two most exalted figures in the history of monasticism, the stable monk is not necessarily the one who can manage to stay in the same place all his life. The stable monk is the one who wants to; and who, left to himself, *would* stay in the same place provided other considerations do not come in to make such local tenure impossible. So long as the monk is not looking for an excuse to waive his stability, all is well. Reasons for securing a transfer of stability from one

142

monastery to another would have to be very strong indeed if the change is to have St. Benedict's blessing upon it. If restlessness alone is the reason, then the probability is that a further change will be sought; and then another. "Never be it thine," counsels Ecclesiasticus, "to bear the reproach of a wanderer. A wretched life it is, passing on from house to house to find a welcome. That welcome found, thou wilt lack all confidence, and sit there mumchance."[1]

We must *abide* in the vine, not merely take our chance in it, or go off to another when we find that to abide is not so easy as we thought. It is true that other vines are of the same species, namely of monasticism and of Christ, and that it is possible for a branch to be taken from one and grafted on to another. But the operation should be rare, and the join always shows. We do not take our vows to a species but to a member of it, not to monasticism but to a monastery.

Discontent and greed are at the bottom of all our faults against stability. Discontent because we are not willing enough to live the life of faith, which finds contentment through discontent; and greed because we hunger for the realization of our dreams. Chronic dissatisfaction with our lot reflects on others besides ourselves, and as much from charity as from stability we should try to find happiness in the monastery to which we belong. It does the wine no good to be decanted from

[1] 29; 31.

one bottle into another; the lees will be there in both bottles, so the safer course is to let the wine settle where it is.

The desire to strike root, to feel the sense of belonging, can amount to a neurosis. Nothing is so unsettling as this desire. It comes between the soul and prayer, it isolates the monk in his own community, it makes steady work if not impossible at least insipid and a great burden. Temptations against stability are apt to be more distracting than temptations against obedience, conversion, and poverty. Stability exists to prevent distraction, not to provoke it. Just as a man joins the monastery knowing that in all probability he will be spared the distraction of want, so in the same way he should join it expecting to be spared the distraction of change.

It is interesting to note that holy Scripture sees instability not only as a psychological handicap, which is the modern view, but as a punishment. "Jerusalem has grievously sinned," we get in Lamentations, "therefore she has become unstable."[2] The curse laid upon Cain for his murder was that he should be "a wanderer upon the earth."[3] The guilty men of Babel were not allowed to settle and be stable. The price that Moses had to pay for his transgression was being kept on the move when above all he wanted to strike roots in the land of

[2] 1; 8.
[3] Gen. 4; 12.

promise. On the other side of the picture we get stability and fixity of tenure hailed as a reward: Josue, at the end, never leaving his tent; Job declaring, in a rare flash of confidence, that he would die in his own place.

Surprising then, after all that is said about it in holy Scripture, that we still evade the implications of stability. In our own particular case there are always conditions, apparently, which make all the difference. Few aspects of the monastic obligation lend themselves so readily to self-deception as stability and conversion of life; yet both of them are matter of vow. To clear the mind of personal bias, natural restlessness, grievance and disillusion, the only way is to submit to the wisdom of authority. If we have not the light, or the faith, to see God's will in the setting of our lives, we surely have the light and faith to know that divine providence is more likely to direct us through our superiors than through any other channel. If in a given instance there are reasons why a monk should leave his monastery for another, God will see to it that these reasons are appreciated by the monk's superiors. Only at the Lord's command did the Hebrews in the desert strike camp; only at the Lord's command did they pitch their tents again, and in the place where he told them to do so. Most of us are part gypsy, part anchorite: we cannot follow both courses, so we tend to be uneasy in the course which is given us to follow. "Winnow not with every wind," says Ecclesiasticus, "and go not into every way."[4] There is a place for winnowing, and this is before the Lord in prayer. There is a particular way for every soul to move in, and if the soul is unprejudiced the way will be made evident. The way will not be made abundantly clear, and certainly it will not be made as attractive as the way which the soul would choose, but at least it will be made evident.

This section on stability may be rounded off with some passages strung together from de Osuna, who, though not himself a Benedictine, shows a sympathetic insight into this cardinal monastic quality. "The second going forth which makes many people restless," he says in the ninth treatise of the work already quoted, "and which further disturbs their peace, is change of place. They mean well by the change, making it because they think it is not the same sun that shines here as there. They believe they will have more spiritual peace if freed from certain annoyances which they suppose they will not find where they are going. But it generally happens that they find things the reverse of what they expected. They are obliged to imitate the large fish bred in fresh water who for the sake of novelty go down to the sea, and when they taste its saltness repent of having left their home and now have to swim back against the stream; for they set out to find peace and have found great want of it; they looked for quiet and saw it was a sham; they sought for angels and found men . . . even

[4] Ch. 5; 11.

when they grow old, such persons are not settled. Wholly wanting in firmness, they are more changeable than the wind or ships without an anchor, or are like trees transplanted in a garden and not yet rooted, and they seek for a time when their souls shall find repose. Of such the prophet Jeremias declares: 'They have loved to move their feet, and have not rested and have not pleased the Lord.' He blames first their moving their feet, and then the result, which is want of the quietude of mind which is the forerunner of the Holy Spirit who is not pleased with those who lack it; this is the final calamity suffered by the unstable . . . I charge you to avoid so far as possible all changes from one province or house to another, for they are a great impediment to recollection, which is not concerned with the locality but with the heart. Remember what our Lord says: 'Whatsoever house ye shall enter into, abide there and depart not thence,' and 'in the same house remain'. . . . If you are ever in doubt as to whether you will go to another locality, I think you should listen to the advice of the wise man who says: 'Trust God, and stay in thy place. For it is easy in the eyes of God on a sudden to make a poor man rich. And the blessing of God makes haste to reward the just man, and in a swift hour his blessing bears fruit.' As a rule devout persons change from one place to another because they think they will profit by it; the wise man tells them to trust that they will advance where they are, and that they should remain there. If they are calm and peaceful, it is easy for God to give them the interior quiescence of grace and the exterior society they desire, if for his honour they substitute for change of abode entrance into themselves and so to be as hidden as possible . . . I have warned people not to wander from place to place, for among a hundred who do so, hardly three will be found who have been actuated by duty or desire of progress, but by some inferior motives. Besides this, those who change of their own accord, especially if they are striving to become recollected and live in peace, meet with difficulties and do not realize what they have lost until too late. If, brother, you wish to practise recollection successfully, do not go forth from yourself, your province, your house, your cell, nor your lips by speaking without evident good results to come. If you do go out, you should be as anxious to return as the fish that gets free from the hook and leaps back to the water."[5]

But stability would be no good without conversion. To keep stability and not to be converted in life and manners would be like keeping enclosure without the will to solitude. The point of stability is to show one's conversion by remaining steadfast in one monastery. The vows hang together: unless there are present also obedience and a turning from the world, stability is no more than residence.

[5] *The Third Spiritual Alphabet*, 8; 3.

Because St. Benedict's second vow is less precise in connotation than the other two, it tends to be more loosely expounded. This is not to say that it is generally less well observed, but that because its meaning is more elusive its observance is less often examined. We tend to examine ourselves more readily on the obvious things, the things we know all about, and to hope for the best about the others. Lacking clear exposition of what this vow exactly involves, and ourselves perhaps failing through laziness to think the thing out, we may go along for years doing the *acts* of our conversion while neglecting to relate them either to the vow or to the abiding state of conversion of heart. There is here a loss not only of merit but of opportunity.

Like stability, conversion of life (or, as it is also called, conversion of manners) is an attitude of mind. Just as stability can be thought of as a fact rather than as a habit, so conversion can be thought of as the act of turning away from the world and not going back on that. But conversion means *keeping on* turning away from the world. All our works as monks should, as they are performed from day to day, bear the mark of this conversion. This should be true not only of our main work, the work to which the community is committed, but also of whatever offices we are called upon to fulfil. Our way of acting should be a converted way, a way quite different from, and sometimes quite opposed to, the way in which people act in the world.

The whole outward framework of monastic life,

whether deriving from the holy Rule itself or from traditional monastic usage, proclaims the difference between living set apart from the world in a religious family and living at home in the world in a natural family. Wearing the habit instead of ordinary clothes, calling one another "Father," "Brother," "Dom," the use of particular terms not current in the world, having one's hair cropped close, having a book read aloud at the two principal meals and observing silence at breakfast and tea, not reading the paper or one's correspondence at breakfast, the times of silence and other duties regulated by the ringing of bells—all these and a hundred other monastic practices are witnesses to conversion and deserve to be cherished as such.

But because a witness to a thing is not the same as the thing itself, the main problem is to make conversion of life an abiding reality. When the inward disposition of conversion has been arrived at and maintained, then all the outward symbols such as we have enumerated become full of meaning and merit. No amount of symbols can do duty for the thing symbolized, but once the substance is present the value of the symbols can be developed indefinitely.

It remains of course always true that where outward signs of inward attitudes are concerned there is the perennial tendency to make an end of what is meant to be either an expression or a means. We can allow to the tonsure or to a certain cut of the habit a moral and

almost mystical value. By itself there is no *virtue* in this
or that habit. It is a piece of material like any other.
The habit is holy only because of the blessing that holiness gives to it—the particular holiness of turning from
the world to God.

Just as the Passion is sacred because Christ suffered
it, the outward forms of monasticism have value only
because of the substance which they represent. Monks
are men who have turned towards Christ. They are so
bent on keeping themselves thus turned that they take
the vow of *conversio* (or *conversatio*) *morum*. From
now on they are pledged to turn away from the world,
and the forms which they use in their new orientation
are indicative of the change. The degree to which the
individual monk is faithful to his vow of conversion
will measure the value of those works, which, without
the life of grace, would have nothing of value to signify.

As the life of prayer develops in the soul, the implications of this second Benedictine vow become
clearer. Where at the beginning it was the negative
side of the ideal—the call to renunciation and unworld-
liness—which made the appeal, now the important
part of it is felt to be the positive turning to God. The
vow and the virtue are seen in terms not so much of
obligation as of opportunity. Conversion may start with
compunction for sin, but it ends in desire for God. The
true fulfilment of this vow is found in the growth of
charity. "If you are wholly converted to the Lord,"

says St. Bernard, "so that you resolve and vow to keep his statutes of perfection, know then that he is himself present, and especially if you feel yourself glowing with the love of him."[6]

If the work of stability is to free the mind of those distractions which come to a man who can move about at will, the work of *conversio morum* is to free the mind of those distractions which come to a man who, in whatever field, is his own master. Thus the second vow strikes deeper than the first. The one opposes self-determination, the other self-love. The first substitutes steadfastness in the one community for the spirit of vagrancy, the second substitutes the love of God for the love of the world. A man who was not a monk might well attain to sanctity without the least call to stability in the accepted monastic sense; he would not attain to sanctity without a radical conversion from worldliness to God. *Conversio morum* is interpreted as "striving after perfection"—a necessary condition, whether in the layman or in the religious, for the crowning grace of sanctity. The *logical* consequence of conversion is the transformation of the unregenerate into the spirit of Christ. That this is often not the *actual* consequence is not the fault of monasticism but of the man.

The monk who is growing in the love of God, whose soul is being prepared by grace for the transforming

[6] *Sermons on the Canticle,* 57.

152

union which is the climax of the life of prayer, is keeping the vow whether he examines himself upon it or not. The whole of his life is a renewal of the vow. Conversion is implicit in everything he does. He does not have to ask himself if this or that is permissible, because if it is something worldly he will not want to permit it. He is facing the other way, and instinctively observes the twentieth instrument of good works, *a saeculi actibus se facere alienum*. The man whose heart is set on living to the full the virtues proposed by his monastic state—charity, humility, obedience, poverty and chastity—will be unworldly in his tastes, in his movements, in his conversation, in his thought.

In considering these three vows ordained by St. Benedict for the training of natural men in the ways of supernatural perfection it is important to see the interior attitude as being responsible for exterior fidelity. The same is of course true in the case of poverty and chastity. If the mind can be so educated by the combined influence of grace, prayer, instruction, and the day-to-day realization of the monastic purpose, as to *think* spiritually—if the mind can be brought to make its judgments in faith—then all the rest follows. By faith the monk will see that he must stay where he is in the monastery of his profession, by faith he will come to widen the gulf which separates him from his worldly self, by faith he will want to submit himself to another in obedience. His poverty and chastity, moreover, will represent his state of mind—acquired again in faith. Since action is conditioned by thought, our fidelity to the vows will depend upon our interior union with God. If we have concluded that the perfection of stability is arrived at through the life of prayer, we can make the same deduction about the perfection of *conversio morum*. It is prayer that opens the eyes of the soul to the graces which are offered by the vows.

Amplifying this idea with particular reference to St. Benedict's third vow, we should see obedience first of all as a blessing and only then as a burden. The emphasis is so often placed upon the "yoke" of obedience that the liberation which obedience effects is sometimes forgotten. While it is true that a man does not take a vow in order to feel more free, it is nevertheless also true that obedience frees a man from the slavery of self-will. Having surrendered his will to another, he is no longer bound by the chains of self-interest. His motives from now onwards, if he is faithful to the ideal of obedience, are selfless. He has chosen not to choose; the choosing is done for him by others.

To the objection that this obedience is a flight from responsibility, a muzzling of freewill, it can be answered that the responsibility is as much there as ever it was but that it is raised to a new level. The responsibility of being faithful to the principles of obedience, and to its countless daily manifestations, is no less great than that of self-direction. Nor is it a curtailing of freewill, but rather an expansion, when the soul spontaneously and deliberately decides to renounce its own rights. There can be nothing cramping about entering more deeply into the will of God. Indeed this is the essence of freedom. We become one with him who makes us free, with him who alone possesses all freedom.

"Man is free," says St. Thomas, "not to do whatever pleases his fancy but what he ought to do by his own free choice. Obedience perfects this freedom, delivering the will from caprice."[7] In the same article St. Thomas explains that while man's will is responsible primarily to the will of God, it is by the will of other men that a man may come to know the will of God, and, by submission to the will of other men, show obedience to it. In the scale of human wills, the will of the subject can give place with confidence to the will of the superior. Whatever merit the subject may lose in renouncing self-chosen acts of generosity is more than compensated for by the willing gift of self.

If we think of religious obedience as existing for the sake of maintaining good order in the monastery, we miss the whole point. Religious authority is something more than a virtuous means of establishing discipline. Religious authority is representative or it is nothing.

[7] *Summa*, II-II, q. 104, 1.

Obedience is something more than the material of a vow; it is a virtue in its own right. It is a virtue which both assumes and expresses other virtues. It proves the quality of other virtues. Charity is tested by obedience and expresses itself in acts of obedience. The same is true of humility. Patience, generosity, hospitality, prayer, penance, fortitude, religious poverty—in fact almost any virtue—can be brought to the bar of obedience for a judgment upon its perfection. St. Thomas teaches that since we owe it in justice to pay homage to God and obey his will, we owe it in justice also to reverence his representatives and obey their wills. Obedience does not stop short at the fulfilment of the command: it is essentially an act of reverence and praise.

Where the stress is laid upon this aspect of praise, suggesting that by our acts of obedience we pay homage to God in the same way that we pay homage to God in choir, the performance of obedience is bound to flow more smoothly than where it is regarded simply as a necessity to be endured in virtue of our vow. The authorities are agreed that obedience is the chief means by which we tend to perfection; it is surrender, it is charity, it is faith.

And because it is so much part of faith, and faith so much part of it, obedience has very often to be given without the least feeling of value or merit. Frequently the acts of obedience are accompanied by a sense of frustration, disgust, and even rebellion. We are not asked to like our obediences, but to perform them for the love of God. So long as we have the intention of fulfilling God's purpose, we can rest assured in faith that the emotional disturbance is not robbing the act of merit or value. "Sensation is sensation," as Dr. Johnson says, "and there's an end of it."

It is interesting, as Fr. Merton notes, to trace the development of teaching in this matter of religious obedience. The desert fathers were anchorites and individualists, so the demand for clear definition was less general than in the later developments of monasticism. A disciple obeyed his master, carrying his obedience sometimes to extreme lengths, because without obedience he was unable to break himself in as a monk. With the spread of the cenobitic ideal, obedience acquired a more positive character. By the time of St. Benedict, obedience had become the primary virtue of the monk and his chief obligation. But it was St. Benedict who developed the doctrine still further by identifying the monk's obedience with the obedience of Christ. For St. Benedict, conformity to the Rule and to the will of the abbot is, according to the degree of purity with which the subject acts, conformity to Christ.

The monk's obedience, then, is single in direction and purpose—the end proposed being the glory of God —but twofold in expression. It is given to the Rule and it is given to the one who commands. Even if the order comes from an equal in the community, it nevertheless represents, in the hierarchy of wills, the will of God. The difficulty arises when there is a discrepancy between the word of the Rule and the word of the ruler. Such a situation calls for much prayer on the part of the superior and subject alike, or the fruit of obedience may well be lost. The light of grace will be needed to determine whether the superior's demand represents a departure from the substance of the Rule or whether the matter of it is only slight. While it is not for the subject to quote the Rule against his superior, neither is it for the superior to take the line *la Règle, c'est moi*. The monk vows his obedience to the Rule and the superior. The superior is as closely bound to the Rule as the subject is bound to it; indeed the superior's responsibility here is greater. "Let all therefore follow the Rule in all things as their guide, and let no man rashly depart from it . . . the abbot himself must do everything with the fear of God and in observance of the Rule, knowing that he will have without doubt to render to God an account of all his judgments."[8]

The subject for his part will need to study the second and third degree of humility, and the sixty-eighth chapter. "That a man love not his own will nor delight in fulfilling his own desires . . . that a man for the love

[8] Ch. 3.

158

of God submit himself to his superior in all obedience,
imitating the Lord, of whom the apostle saith 'He was
made obedient unto death' . . . if on any brother there
be laid commands that are hard and impossible, let
him receive the orders of him who commands with all
docility; but if he sees that the weight of the burden
altogether exceeds his strength, then let him with
patience lay before his superior the reasons for his
incapacity to obey, showing neither pride, resistance,
nor contradiction. If after this the superior still persist
in his command, let the subject know that it is expedient for him. And let him obey for the love of God,
trusting in his help."

For some it is an abiding trial right through their
religious lives that they should look for a solution to
this kind of problem and never find it. How square the
letter and principles of the Rule with its current interpretation and practice? Do stability and obedience between them close the gap? The bewildered soul, with
St. Benedict's text there in front of him, cannot find it
in him to be sure that they do. For him now, as for all
of us always, the only course is prayer in faith. "We
have no strength of our own to meet such an onslaught
as this," the soul can cry with the author of Parali-
pomena, "we, despairing hearts that know not where
else to turn, we look to thee."[9] It is not always failure
in the spirit of obedience and stability that makes a

[9] II Par. 20; 12.

monk unhappy in his monastery and difficult for an abbot to help or handle; it is more often failure to see where the only possible help can come from. Prayer in faith.

If those in authority allowed themselves to be guided by the text "Look well, and make everything in due accord with the pattern that was given thee on the mount,"[10] and if those under them took more seriously to heart the fifty-seventh instrument of good works, "to apply oneself frequently to prayer," the ideal of obedience would present fewer practical problems and occasion less searching of heart. We are prone enough as it is to introspection; to provide new reasons for self-examination is surely foreign to our Benedictine inheritance. As it stands in the holy Rule, the doctrine seems so simple—"that a man love not his own will, nor delight in fulfilling his own desires"—but when it comes to the question of living by that standard it is, both for the superior and for the subject, a business of some complexity. Obedience, whether looking down from the height of authority or looking up from the level of subjection, admits of only one mode of approach—namely, faith.

When we come to the subject of poverty we are on less specifically Benedictine ground. This is not to claim that obedience is a Benedictine prerogative, but merely to suggest that where in the case of obedience

[10] Exod. 25; 40.

St. Benedict gives his own very clear instructions as to how it is to be performed, in the case of poverty both the manner in which the obligation is to be fulfilled and the degree of renunciation and actual need have largely to be inferred. St. Benedict assumes religious poverty, referring to what the monk may reasonably have for his use in the way of clothes, bedding, and personal belongings, but he does not give to poverty the same individual character that he gives to stability and obedience.

The danger for a Benedictine, therefore, in attempting to explain his poverty, is the danger of explaining it away. Monastic poverty may not be the same as that suffered by the indigent in the world, may not be that of the mendicant friars, but it has a distinct meaning and must play a real part in the life. Those who say that poverty in the Benedictine sense begins and ends with the idea of detachment from personal possessions talk nonsense. Benedictine history has shown that in periods when the monastic tradition has stood highest, poverty has been most strictly interpreted. That the due practice of poverty must *lead* to detachment from personal possessions, and that this is one of the main objects in cultivating it, is obvious enough. What is not so generally understood is that the virtue is inseparable from the fact, and that the fact must have an actual and not a legal or theoretical existence. Monastic poverty, in short, means doing without.

Many different elements go to make up the ideal of monastic poverty. There is the principle of holding all things in common and so eliminating as far as possible the vices of greed, *proprietas* or private ownership, envy of others, display, patronage, and inequality in the standard of living within the monastery. But the most important aspect of it lies in the likeness to Christ which it brings out in the soul. Having all possessions laid before him, Christ chose to be without possessions.

If identification with Christ is at the heart of religious obedience, it is at the heart of religious poverty no less. It is not denudation for the sake of denudation; it is rather oblation in union with Christ's oblation, sacrifice in union with Christ's sacrifice. It is difficult to see how such an attitude of mind can be developed in the monk without actual renunciations, without positive attempts being made to reproduce something of the condition of life in which Christ lived. When allowance has been made for economic, racial, social and other differences, there is still in every generation and in every civilization the standard of the working man. Monasteries do not have to model themselves on slums, but they should have at least some features in common with working-class households. If they have not, then the term poverty can have very little meaning.

On the above showing, and getting down now to practical expressions of the obligation, it would be difficult to justify such things as membership of a club, the use of hired cars when cheaper transport is available, lodging at expensive hotels when away from the monastery, treating oneself or others to expensive meals, subscribing to newspapers and magazines. Though the use of tobacco appears incongruous against the poverty of Nazareth, the incongruity is a little softened in the setting of the contemporary workman's cottage. Smoking, like playing golf, is one of those indulgences which touch *conversio morum* as much as they touch poverty. Indeed, since most of the offences against poverty are offences against conversion, the one vow can be checked by the other.

Monastic poverty is so much the sign of conversion from the world that half the monastic practices which point to simplicity of life find their inspiration in conversion and their expression in poverty. The multiplicity and extravagance of the world are countered in the monastery by usages designed to suggest unsophistication, unconcern with the fetishes of society, unfashionable standards, unluxurious taste. In some monasteries, for example, it is the custom to serve the coffee or tea already mixed and sweetened, to provide the same allowance of butter, jam, cheese, or whatever it may be on the plate before the brethren arrive in the refectory, to allot a particular time in the day for bedmaking, shoe-cleaning, cell-sweeping. Treating men like children? Kindergarten rules? Primitive? Possibly, but it must be remembered that St. Benedict compares the monastery both to a school and to a workshop. Perhaps the only way to resist the evils of excessive modernity is to live a little primitively, a little more simply than is strictly necessary. Certainly the monk who has the true spirit of poverty will exercise the working man's thrift in the use of light, fuel, food, clothes, tools, stamps and paper.

To this it might be objected that if such a standard of comparison is chosen, the typewriter is as out of place in the labourer's cottage as the cigar. If editors and publishers were less insistent on typescript the objection would be valid, but it is here submitted that the typewriter is to the Benedictine what the tractor is to the Cistercian and what the car or motor-bicycle is to the missionary. There is a difference between using a typewriter which is a tool and a television set which is a toy.

Those who seem to see in monastic poverty nothing more than a medieval fad, and a rather hypocritical fad at that, should bear in mind that exactly half the monastic purpose is to detach the will from the desire of material things. How else than by the spirit and practice of religious poverty can the monk show that his happiness is placed beyond the reach of earthly possessions? Poverty is a standing evidence to the truth that men can find their true joy in God alone and not alone in his gifts. If our treasure really is in heaven, then the rust and the moth can do their worst. God has granted the grace of detachment.

But even when this has been said, the merits of religious poverty are still not exhausted. Added to the personal poverty of the monk there is the blessing of charity which comes from the common practice of poverty in the monastery. In the instance given above it is the common life as well as the simple life that is aimed at. Equality in food, regularity in details of household timetable, uniformity in dress—these things are meant to provide a bond as well as a discipline. Since so many of the good things that the monastic life has to offer can be harmed by singularity, by fastidiousness, by the tricks of private ambition and policy, by isolationism and self-direction, it is poverty's great merit that with obedience it can act in the monastery as a leveller. We need to be as level as possible if we are to be one in charity.

If the poverty of the apostles, as it was pointed out by Fr. Middendorf at a recent congress of religious in Rome, was devised to give greater liberty for the preaching of the Gospel, the chastity of religious has a parallel function. Where poverty brings the soul to dependence upon divine providence, chastity brings the soul to a concentration of the affections upon divine love. Where poverty makes it easier for the Holy Spirit to reach, through the detached will of a man, the souls of other men, chastity makes it easier for the Holy Spirit, through the undivided heart of a man, both to reach the hearts of others and to perfect the work of grace in the man himself.

Though monastic chastity may have been introduced originally to curb wrongful desires, it does not exist for this alone. It exists to develop rightful desires, and to train them upon God. The mistake is to think of chastity as a holy discipline and not as a holy state; to think of it as smothering the affections instead of sanctifying them.

While matrimony and monasticism alike raise human love to a divine level, they do not raise it in the same way. Matrimony works through the physical body of individuals, monasticism through the common body of the community. The matrimonial state makes holy the natural union, the monastic state makes holy the celibate condition. Each state is governed by its own rules, produces its own responsibilities, has its own joys. Just as in the natural family the members are not isolated units who happen to be living under the same roof, so in the supernatural family the members have a similar social obligation. In both cases, matrimonial and monastic, this obligation is contradicted by infidelity. Unchastity at once pulls down the ideal. Pulls down not *both* ideals, but the *one* ideal—because the common ideal is that of charity.

Marriage is a sacrament not *only* to guard fallen nature against itself; it is a sacrament primarily because it reflects the union of Christ with his Church. When the Church is called the Bride of Christ, it is not as though man's symbols were borrowed to typify something divine. It is not as though divine revelation had to wait upon metaphors coined by man, but rather that man's ideas are shaped according to the pattern revealed by God.

Monastic chastity is observed, therefore, not merely in *honour* of the virginity of Christ and of his mother, but as a symbol of divine love itself. Since the truest love is self-sacrificing love—is the love of Christ for the Father and for the Church—the love which the monastic life sets out to perfect must be chaste. If conversion of life is defined as the continued pursuit of perfection, chastity follows as a necessary consequence. By conversion and poverty a monk leaves all earthly things behind him in order to live more perfectly to Christ; by chastity he identifies his power of love with Christ's love, and so proves the quality of his single-mindedness. Body and spirit are acting in harmony, in a holy complicity which expresses the highest generosity.

Virginity of body is an excellence for which the monk should never cease to show gratitude to God; it is a good which, in sacrifice, he can refer back again to God. He can know that such an offering cannot but give praise to God. But he must know at the same time that the value of what he offers is conditioned by the spirit in which he offers it. It is virginity of heart and soul that supremely matters: chastity of outlook, of mind, of desire.

As in the case of stability and obedience, the obligation of chastity is proved by an increasing attention to detail but does not consist in attention to detail. It consists in a purity which mounts from the rejection of impurity to the extension and sanctification of love. In the course of this process the side of sex which appeals to human appetite becomes less of a practical threat to the soul's perfection, and the side of it which alone appeared before the fall is more clearly understood.

The virtue is called the "holy" virtue, but it is not likely to advance in holiness without the practice both of discipline and prayer. The monastic life may provide some of the safeguards, but it does not guarantee to do the work either of saving or of sanctifying. Enclosure, manual labour, the example of the brethren, and above all the access to the sacraments and the daily sacrifice of the Mass—everything is there. A great part of the obligation of chastity is to make use of the protections with which the monk is surrounded. If seclusion and the rules of the monastery to a certain extent cut off the occasions of sin, it is only in the cultivation of the prayer life and the eucharistic life that the virtue positively develops. Orientating his spirituality towards the Blessed Sacrament, drawing his strength from the Mass, the monk comes inevitably to want what Christ wants and to live in the state that Christ lives. Life in Christ, which is no trick of the imagination but solid theological fact, is the solution to the problem of chastity and the only way of keeping the vow.

In the last analysis, then, it must be again faith that carries the soul through to the perfection of the virtue. Always there is the same struggle between what we know we should want and what we feel we must have. However certain the mind, the senses have great power to disturb. Sometimes the senses cause such disturbance as to shake the certainty of the mind: the soul begins to doubt whether the appetites have not gained complete control. Now more than ever is there need of faith— faith in the power of grace, in the mercy of God, and in the knowledge that neither temptation, emotion, nor sensation constitutes sin. In each of the vows, but perhaps more immediately in the case of chastity, faith plays the controlling part. Where in regard to the other virtues the need is more for the habit, in regard to chastity the need is often for the imperative act. Why are we fearful? Why are our hearts troubled? Only because we are men of little faith. This is the victory, on each occasion as well as in the final issue, our faith.

When St. Benedict tells his monks in the sixty-third instrument of good works "to love chastity," he is giving the principle which equally governs stability, conversion, obedience, and poverty. If we do not love the virtue which is responsible for the works, we shall perform the works lifelessly and end by not performing them at all. In the same fourth chapter St. Benedict says we are to "love fasting . . . not to love much speaking . . . to hate one's own will . . . not to love strife." The whole thing lies in the mental approach: wanting what the Rule proposes, not wanting what it forbids. To take up the other attitude is at once to establish a frontier and to build a system of defence. The legal demand is admitted, but advance into the heart, into the essential self, is denied. "You may have my service," says the monk who has failed to learn the secret of monastic happiness, "but not my mind." Such a monk regards himself as bound in honour but not in love. The monastery is entitled to his time, to whatever works he may produce, even to his body. He has vowed himself, and he does not think of going back on that. "But you shall not invade that area," he says in effect, "which must for ever belong to me, and to me alone." He takes part in what is ordained by monasticism, but he is not identified with the will that gives life to monasticism.

The force which keeps the religious life together is not the system of the vows but the response to love. Love must have its sanctions, but it is not the sanctions that constitute the love. Love is constituted, is animated, by itself. Love is the only absolute because God himself is love. Love works through the vows; monasticism works through the vows. Where love is perfect, as it is in heaven, there is no need for either vows or monasticism. Meanwhile love, vows, monasticism—conditioned by grace and worked out in faith—draw together in the one direction and find their object in God. Without love, the vows would be unendurable and monasticism would be pointless; with love, the vows are so much worship and monasticism is the way of happiness as well as the way of perfection.

10

The Consequences
of Fidelity

JUST AS THE ARTIST, to the extent that he follows his
particular art, tends to think in the terms of that art,
so the monk, to the extent that he follows the grace of
his vocation, tends to think in the terms of that vocation. The artist's vision and judgment come to him by
the combined influence of knowledge, experience, in-
tuition; the monk's by training and grace. In neither
case do the critical faculties have to be brought to bear.
Except for occasions when the critical faculties are ex-
pressly called upon for approval or condemnation, the
mind operates according to the movement which is
habitual. Whatever the aspect of beauty it is that
moulds the artist's thought, the aspect that moulds the
thought of the monk is at once spiritual and practical.
Monastic life is not a dream but a reality; it is lived
on both planes at once. Monasticism is not an ideal
only; it is a way. Neither aesthetic nor abstract beauty
is the object of the monk's search. The monk is looking
for a beauty which is moral and supernatural, which
can be discovered on earth and perfectly possessed only

in heaven. The monk can find what he is looking for only in Christ.

Monastic life is a beginning, a becoming. It does not pretend to be anything more. It proposes a constant renewal, demanding of the soul a willingness to persevere in the light of what is shown by grace. God gives to the soul at the beginning the merest glimpse of what it is all about—just enough to arouse the soul's desire and to elicit the response which God is looking for. And then, as the horizon widens, the quality of the surrender undergoes a change. "It is one thing to see the land of peace from the forest ridge," says St. Augustine, "and another to tread the road that leads to it."[1] The quality of the surrender is in the treading. The land of peace drops out of sight. The soul wonders whether the land of peace was ever really seen. Whether it exists at all. Other lands invite inspection. As the going gets rougher the heart sinks lower. There is nothing left but the original purpose—no glimpse any more, or zest—but it is precisely this fidelity to the naked purpose that is the essence of the whole life, that is the proof of it. It is the life of faith.

Much of the work of religion, and therefore more particularly of monasticism, is to keep the soul faithful to the light of grace when the sense of grace has been removed. We are men fallen from original grace; inconstancy and disillusion are in our blood. Sometimes

[1] Confessions, 7; 21.

174

because our natures are roused by an objective stimulus, sometimes for no apparent reason at all, we feel like throwing everything over and abandoning God altogether. It is the restless blood of our first parents quickening in our veins. But with this goes always the grace of *not* throwing everything over, of *not* abandoning God. The truth is that he refuses to abandon us. It is his tenacity, not ours, that is our fidelity. Our strong-mindedness is not the cause of our perseverance; his love is the cause of our perseverance.

Lex Dei ejus in corde ipsius, et non supplantabuntur gressus ejus.[2] God pledges himself to remain with the man who keeps the divine law in his heart. The steps of such a man will move in the right way because God will be his impulse and support. I remain faithful, now not I, but God remains faithful for me. If in me he has his unrestricted will, he is remaining faithful to himself. My feet shall not stray because they are his, and Christ walks always towards the Father. The Pauline doctrine of divine indwelling, of identification with Christ, raises the whole idea of Christian observance from the strictly legal to the strictly supernatural plane. The whole idea of monastic observance is accordingly translated from outward service to service of the highest spiritual significance.

The second clause in the verse quoted from the thirty-sixth psalm supposes the verification of the first.

[2] Psalm 36; 31.

175

If the law of God is not in the heart, there is no guarantee that the work of grace will be so fruitful. When the man grows casual about the law of God, when he has no longer God's will at heart, his steps move easily from the right way. As the Christian has no right to presume upon the promises and protection of the Gospel unless he lives according to the Gospel, so the monk has no right to presume upon the promises and protection of the Rule unless he lives according to the Rule.

The Christian who disregards the claims of Christ or of the Church is virtually associating himself with those who cry, "Away with him . . . we will not have this man to rule over us." The monk who disregards the claims of St. Benedict or of the abbot is virtually associating himself in the same way with those who cry, "Away with him." If while still appearing to be a Christian a man can be a rebel against the name of Christ, so while appearing to be a monk a man can be a rebel against monasticism. Explicitly the cry may not be raised, "We will not have St. Benedict to rule over us . . . we will not have an abbot to rule over us," but there are times when the words are implicit in the attitude and action of monks.

In the course of the holy Rule there are few passages more rich in implication than that on which the final chapter closes. "Whoever thou art that hastens towards thy heavenly country, fulfil by Christ's help this least of Rules which we have written for beginners; and then at length thou shalt arrive, under God's protection, at the lofty summits of doctrine and virtue of which we have told you." Hastening, always beginners, trusting wholly in God: it is all there. Nor is the doctrine that St. Benedict gives us—and he gives us a good deal of it in his seventy-three chapters—pure doctrine and nothing else. Everywhere it is doctrine related to virtue. Always it must be the pursuit of the virtue that proves the acceptance of the doctrine.

Commenting on St. Paul's determination to stretch forth himself to those things that lie before, St. Augustine says that "the life of a good Christian is nothing but a desire." St. Augustine might have been writing specifically for monks when he goes on: "That which you desire, you do not yet see. But by the act of desiring you will be made capable of containing to the full that which you will see when it comes. By deferring it, God increases our desire; and by our desire our heart is sufficiently enlarged. Let us then desire, since we are to be filled. This is our life, that by desiring we may be qualified. And holy desires will qualify us in proportion as we curb our longing for this world's love." Monasticism exists for this: to curb the monk's longing for one kind of love and to draw it towards another.

Quaerite Dominum, et confirmamini; quaerite faciem ejus semper.[3] Spiritual writers tell of two ways by which we seek after God: in general by faith, and in particular

[3] Psalm 104; 4.

by prayer. Seeking God in the exercise of our faith is our first duty as Christians; seeking him by recollection is our added duty as monks. "We have to search for the presence of the Lord," to quote St. Augustine once again, "which, though it is found by faith, we must continue to search for in this life so that hereafter we may find it by presence."

Earlier in this book mention was made of three requisites demanded by Francisco de Osuna for the work of contemplation. Two of these we have already discussed. The third, as bringing our theme to its logical conclusion, we can consider here. "Of those things chiefly required for quiet, recollected contemplation, besides many others which may be useful," says de Osuna, "the third is the preparation and disposition of our will, which by the grace of God we must always keep in readiness like wax to be stamped with the seal. Some people resemble honeycombs without the honey, but in the recollected man this [the honey] should never be wanting. He should strive to keep it ever in his heart and will, like the bride who said, 'My soul melted when he spoke.' The will must be very soft and tender if it is to melt at a word, and even less than a word but at simply having heard him speak without knowing what was said . . . therefore keep your will free from malice and adorned with tenderness of heart, for the peace of God is promised to men of good will . . . our whole spiritual progress consists in the disposition and preparation of our will, and this good will is the means by which grace is given us . . . the three things mentioned help the soul greatly to reach God peacefully. But the third is the most essential."[4] (It will be remembered that the first requirement was a suitable place for prayer, and the second an opportunity for mixing with contemplative souls.)

In the above passage there is a reference which, if not properly understood, might prove misleading. The terms "honey," "tenderness," "melting" are not to be pressed. From what the author says elsewhere it is clear that the doctrine makes no bid for sensible devotion. What de Osuna wants of the soul is not sweetness, which in any case it is not often in the soul's power to have, but receptivity. For the soul to respond instantly to the breathing of the spirit there need be no emotional reaction whatever. Certainly the response is proved not by the intensity of feeling but by the fidelity with which the grace is followed up.

"Do not lightly believe that you cannot practise re-collection," says the same de Osuna, "for though there may be many obstacles the will, aided by grace and a relish for interior contemplation, can override them all . . . our Lord calls you at the gate of your consent; it is for you to open your desire. The dove, which is the gift of the Holy Ghost, comes to the ark of your

[4] *Third Spiritual Alphabet,* 15; ch. 6.

heart; it is for you to put forth the hand of love and take it in."[5]

If the soul is to be disposed to receive the grace of contemplation, the need for recollection outside the set periods of prayer is absolute. To expect the gift without having taken the trouble to prepare the way for the gift would be to act with presumption. For a monk to expect that he will reach the heights to which his vocation calls him would be again, unless his hope is backed by the serious effort to practise recollection, presumption. Since the monastic life proposes the life of faith, and since the life of faith is developed in the setting of recollection, monastic perfection supposes the practice of recollection.

"It is of such immense advantage for us to cultivate the habit of recollection," says St. Teresa, "that you must not be surprised at my mentioning it very frequently. Do not be disturbed if you do not succeed at first. Perhaps the devil may be filling your heart with repugnance and trouble because he sees what loss he would suffer by your acquiring the habit . . . our Lord tests your love for himself, and if he sees that our works conform to our words he will not fail to grant our prayers, to aid us with supernatural graces such as the prayer of quiet, perfect contemplation and other favours."[6]

[5] *Ibid.*, pp. 308-9.
[6] *Camino*, chs. 36, 37.

If our study of the holy Rule has taught us nothing else than to see in its appointments and regulations the underlying principles of prayer and faith, we shall have grasped the main issues. Observance is worship in faith; the vows are worship in faith; the threefold service of work, reading, the divine office is worship in faith. Fidelity in the monastic state amounts to no more and no less than this, and if we have insisted throughout this book on the necessity of keeping to the word of our holy Father it has been simply because his voice speaks to us from the depths of his recollection. The letter of the holy Rule is important because it is conceived in the spirit. It is in terms of St. Benedict's spirit that the letter of his Rule is understood. But it is also true to say that we cannot come to know his spirit without an experimental study of his terms.

As St. Benedict's abbot must "be learned in the law of God, that he may know whence to bring forth new things and old,"[7] so St. Benedict's monks must be willing learners of the holy Rule, that they may see the connection between new things and old. Without prayer and a study of our holy Father's thought there is always the danger either of letting the modern depart too far from the standard set by the original or of failing to make allowance for new things which must necessarily rise out of the old. The good zeal which St. Benedict wants to see in his monks—the zeal "which keeps

[7] Ch. 64.

us from vice and which leads us to God and to life everlasting"[8]—should incline us to endure with patience not only one another's infirmities but also the differences of interpretation between monk and monk, monastery and monastery, generation and generation. *Hunc ergo zelum ferventissimo amore exerceant monachi, id est ut honore se invicem praeveniant.*[9] By deferring to others, by respecting the views put forward in other ages of Benedictine history as well as those put forward by other Benedictines in our own age, we at least learn to practise humility. If this is so, it has St. Benedict's blessing upon it.

[8] Ch. 72.
[9] *Ibid.*